OPERATIONAL EMPOWERMENT

COLLABORATE, INNOVATE, AND ENGAGE TO BEAT THE COMPETITION

SHAWN CASEMORE

New York Chicago San Francisco Athens London
Madrid Mexico City Milan New Delhi
Singapore Sydney Toronto

1 2 3 4 5 6 7 8 9 0   DOC/DOC   1 2 1 0 9 8 7 6 5

ISBN 978-1-259-58791-7
MHID   1-259-58791-6

e-ISBN 978-1-259-58792-4
e-MHID   1-259-58792-4

Library of Congress Cataloging-in-Publication Data

Casemore, Shawn, author.
   Operational empowerment : collaborate, innovate, and engage to beat the competition / Shawn Casemore.
      pages cm
   ISBN 978-1-259-58791-7 (alk. paper) — ISBN 1-259-58791-6 (alk. paper)
      1. Industrial management.   2. Production management.   I. Title.
   HD31.2.C37 2016
   658—dc23   2015028855

McGraw-Hill Education books are available at special quantity discounts to use as premiums and sales promotions or for use in corporate training programs. To contact a representative, please visit the Contact Us pages at www.mhprofessional.com.

To my wife, Julie, for her patience; my boys, Matthew and Dylan, for their constant inspiration, and to my clients, for your confidence and unwavering support.

Contents

Part 3: Collaborative Power

Part 4: Capturing and Capitalizing on Innovation

Acknowledgments

There are three people without whom I would likely not have written this book. Alan Weiss, the author of over 50 books in 12 languages and *the* thought leader in solo consulting, continues to challenge me to realize what is possible. Without Alan's guidance and support I likely wouldn't be where I am today. Chad Barr, a technological guru and author in his own right, provided immense support in framing my ideas for this book, and Colleen Francis, a colleague and friend, provided continued encouragement and support.

Thank you to my editor, Knox Huston. Your confidence in me and my ideas was a constant motivation to keep me moving forward.

Thank you to Esmond Harmsworth, my agent, who was the first to believe that how I help clients today is something that would be beneficial for all to know.

Lastly, thank you to my wife and business partner, Julie. Your constant support and belief in me inspires me to do more and be more, each and every day.

Introduction

Have you ever wondered what differentiates a highly productive operation from one whose performance is less than efficient or effective? What are the factors that contribute to maximizing the performance, accuracy, and profitability demonstrated by one organization's operations over its competitors? If, for example, you consider the volume of popular literature that exists on business management, then you might believe that leadership is the single greatest contributing factor to maximizing the effectiveness of an operation—however, you'd be only partially correct.

Some of the most popular business leaders of our time like Herb Kelleher, former CEO of Southwest Airlines, or Tony Hsieh, CEO of the online shoe and clothing store Zappos.com, do stand above the crowd when it comes to their approach to leadership; however, the key differentiator is not in what they do, but what they don't do. Their focus is not on managing, but instead *empowering their people*. What makes an operation effective is the ability of the employees within the operation to continuously collaborate, be creative, and act upon ideas to improve how the business operates without the encouragement, enticement, or direction of management. Empowerment is the key, and if formulated and nurtured correctly, it will sustain long after management has left the building.

During my career I have had the good fortune of working with some of the top performing organizations in the world, including Magna International, the largest auto parts supplier in North America, and consumer products giant Pepsi Co. In my corporate career, I also had the experience of working for organizations that were struggling to achieve the levels of performance and profitability they desired, includ-ing Fortune 500 auto parts company Meritor Suspension Systems and electronics leader NCR. Interestingly, I've learned that the factors that separate high-performing organizations from those that struggle are not as complex and costly as we often believe them to be. More specifically, what differentiates high-performing operations from those that falter is not the technology; it's not the capital resources available; it's not the market or industry; and it's not the geographic location.

Consider for a moment the organizations that your company com-petes with today, and it will be readily apparent that the technology, equipment, and suppliers that are engaged to create or deliver your products or services are relatively the same as those of your closest com-petitor. If they aren't, it's likely that they will be before long. Therefore there is only one key contributor that allows an organization to differen-tiate in its market and maximize competitive advantage, and that differ-entiator is people. Put another way, the profit and performance power of an organization resides solely in the hands of the employees that operate the business on a daily basis (Figure I.1). They can, in essence, make or break a company.

FIGURE I.1 Performance vs. Profit

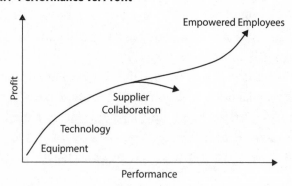

Consider a widely recognized (and profitable) organization that is known for capitalizing on the power of its employees, like Stanley Black & Decker. With a vast array of salable products such as com-plex tools and power equipment, Black & Decker realized a significant disconnect existed between product design, manufacturing, and sales. To enhance the design and functionality of its products, Black & Decker instituted the use of video to allow sales representatives to provide detailed and timely feedback on exactly how products were being used in the field. This was a simple yet effective means of empowering the sales representatives and the designers and manufacturers of Black & Decker products to communicate and initiate changes that further supported end user application. Stanley Black & Decker has solidified its market dominance and sustained growth despite steadily increasing competition because it realized the value in empowering its employees to make timely decisions and take actions to ensure that operations are both efficient and customer centric.[1]

Engaging with employees is not only valuable to generate product and service innovation, it is also essential to incrementally and continuously improve organizational performance. Employees hold the ideas, knowledge, and power to transform a company from mediocre performance to high performance. This is the essence of *Operational Empowerment*: building a framework and community that will transform how your business operates from average performance to extraordinary performance.

In this book we will explore the operational components required to build and sustain a perpetually profitable business model through varying forms of collaboration and engagement. We will begin in Part 1 by building a foundation for empowerment in order to capitalize on what I call the *power of the people*. With the proper foundation in place, in Part 2 we will explore how to engage employees in formulating and achieving a future vision for the organization with focus and sustained intensity. In Part 3 we will introduce and discuss the tools that will enhance employee empowerment and maximize the speed and agility of the organization. Finally, in Part 4, we will discuss how to ensure that these new levels of operational performance are both repeatable and sustainable.

Throughout the book we will discuss examples of companies that have successfully adopted these concepts and approaches to maximize their operational performance, companies like one of my longstanding clients, Gerson and Gerson. As a manufacturer of children's garments,

Gerson and Gerson has a historic reputation for providing quality garments, but in order to compete in a broadening and price-sensitive market, G&G has evolved into a very complex business model. In order to capitalize on the power of its employees and increase its competitive advantage, G&G sought to empower its employees to introduce change and improvement. We will spend time reviewing G&G's journey and how the company transformed itself into a more competitive and empowered operation to thrive in a very competitive marketplace.

We will also spend time discussing exactly how the techniques and concepts outlined in *Operational Empowerment* transcend across all industries, sectors, and businesses by exploring organizations like Vokes Furniture Incorporated, a second-generation family-owned business that, despite multiple attempts to find and integrate a general manager to oversee company operations, was only able to realize the higher levels of productivity and improved morale desired when it shifted away from a formal management hierarchy and instead empowered its employee teams to manage daily operations.

I will caution you that this book is not meant as a quick fix or a Band-Aid to improve your existing operational performance, although there are hundreds of ideas contained within it that will support a rapid and slightly less robust approach to achieving just that. This book is meant as a road map to building and sustaining high levels of productivity and profitability. It will challenge your existing beliefs and debunk much of common day theory on how business operations should be structured and managed in order to maximize operational performance.

If your desire is to dramatically improve profitability, productivity, and morale, then *Operational Empowerment* is the solution you have been seeking. Let the journey begin!

—Shawn Casemore
On board a flight to New York City
June 2015

Join the Operational Empowerment Community!

This book is meant as a playbook to help CEOs and executives structure and build a more empowered business, improving productivity and profitability. The book, however, is only the beginning, providing a launching pad upon which you can further evolve and improve the structure and effectiveness of your operation.

As with any change, additional resources and ongoing support are necessary in order to ensure success. One of the most significant factors that will ensure your success in improving the effectiveness of your operation is by sharing, collaborating, and learning with peers.

It's for this reason that I've compiled numerous resources, education, programs, tools, and ongoing support to help you and your team become more operationally empowered. You can tap into these tools by visiting www.operationalempowerment.com, where you will find resources that include:

1. **Join our online community**
   Connect with other people reading the book and pursuing the empowerment of their operation. Ask questions, share solutions, and increase the velocity of your results.
2. **Learn more about the approaches discussed**
   Find resources, checklists, models, and tools to help you ensure a successful transition to a fully empowered operation.
3. **Do the work**
   Download PDFs of a variety of exercises from the book to fill out on your own, or to print out and distribute to your team.

4. **Download an Empowered Executive Coaching Guide**

   Want to learn how to coach your team to adopt an empowered approach? Learn how CEOs and executives can integrate empowered coaching and mentoring practices in order to build a stronger, more empowered team.

5. **Exclusive access**

   The material in this book documents the experiences that I have with my clients each and every day. As I find new material, insights, and opportunities, I will share them with you to help you continue to evolve the empowerment in your operation.

   Visit www.operationalempowerment.com to dive deeper into forming your own empowered operation.

PART 1

The Infliction of Poor Operational Performance

In the speaking and consulting I have done with CEOs and executives from around the world, I've spent considerable time finding ways to help companies improve their operational performance.

To my dismay, however, in most instances the foundational aspects of building a high-performing business operation are often insufficient or missing altogether, mostly because of incorrect information and archaic business practices that have long since lost their effect.

In Part 1 of this book, I will share with you the fundamental reasons why we are failing to achieve high-performing operations despite the input of significant energy and investments. Most importantly, I will present the key ingredients for establishing a foundation upon which a high-performing operation can be built, allowing you the opportunity to create renewed and lasting improvements that will span decades and leave your competition in the dust.

1

The Power Is in the People

Misconceptions That Reduce Operational Performance

There are some foundational flaws in how most businesses operate today. Our perceptions of "reducing" costs, "managing" employees, and "introducing" innovation are founded on business fundamentals that were created decades ago. We are trying to increase productivity and profitability using an out-of-date business model that was never intended to engage the culturally diversified and technologically advanced society that we live in today. Shifts in how our employees, suppliers, contractors, and customers (the people that support a business) prefer to be engaged are becoming more apparent as baby boomers retire and millennials become the more dominant and influential generation.

This shift is readily apparent in the consumer services sector, where less bureaucracy and a smaller workforce have resulted in faster-evolving and more recognizable change. My doctor, for example, retired at the age of 70. He was the epitome of old school. On the wall of his office was a handwritten paper sign that read "Conversations beyond 20 minutes will result in a fee of $100 being applied to your bill. Any conversations that last less than 20 minutes are considered complimentary." He was a doctor, but his perceptions of how to "manage" patients were quite different from those of doctors of today's younger generation. I experienced this firsthand when he retired and a new doctor, some 40 years younger, took over his practice. The new doctor relocated the practice to a new office, consolidating his practice with that of six other family doctors. The staff he chose worked collaboratively with other doctors, allowing for a seamless patient experience in which doctors can actually serve increased numbers of patients due to the communication and information sharing across various practices. Most surprisingly, during every appointment he takes the time to ask questions and he seems to genuinely enjoy engaging in discussion. There are no signs, verbal or visual, that set limits to discussion and diagnosis. My new doctor's approach to client care and management represents a common evolution in patient care, shifting from a business-focused to a patient-focused model.

This example of shifting influences in a consumer setting mimics what we find in the corporate world, where an archaic business model that is focused on a top-down, cost-driven, convoluted structure has created gaps and obstacles between business leaders, employees, suppliers, and customers. Put another way, we are applying a flawed business model to how we operate companies today, the essence of which is longstanding interpretations of how to best structure, manage, and lead organizations in order to maximize productivity.

The first and most significant flaw of this model is the *management hierarchy*. Originally derived for military purposes, a management hierarchy was based on the notion that there was either a "hierarchy" of management or "anarchy" among the people. A hierarchy is built on the premise that in order to have hundreds of employees do as needed (and instructed), it is necessary to *enforce* a directional management style, which starts from the top and travels downward throughout the organization. This may have worked well to suit the purposes of the military, but it has done little more than create a distinct divide between business leadership and employees, otherwise known as "us" versus "them." The concept of a hierarchy in and of itself promotes a top-down approach to leading, managing, and communicating with employees, squashing out any opportunities to have a meaningful dialogue.

The next most significant flaw in business operations that we see today is our approach to *leadership*. Building on the management hierarchy mentioned earlier, we build "troops" in the form of frontline supervision, middle management, and senior management; then we invest time, energy, and resources into developing managers' abilities as if this alone will serve to increase engagement with employees. In fact, organizations are so convinced of the value of this investment that in North America alone the spending in annual training and development is near 60 billion dollars. I'm not suggesting the flaw is in the investment itself, but rather in *how* money is invested. The very notion of investing heavily in company leadership while ignoring or minimizing the development needs of employees is ludicrous, yet considering the premise of the "management hierarchy," it's clear why this decision may have come about. If employee productivity is not as we desire, a management hierarchy leads us to the assumption that an *investment in the people who lead our employees* must be in order. This is like buying a new engine for your car when your tires are worn out. An investment is necessary, but it's misdirected and won't help you reach your destination any faster or with any greater efficiency.

The last fundamental flaw in how businesses operate today is in our approach to *employee communications*. We communicate to employees on a "need to know" basis. The larger the organization seems, the more employees feel like mushrooms—kept in the dark and fed less-than-appetizing nutrients. Building on the perceptions of how to effectively "lead our people," communications travel from the top down, forming a one-directional approach to communications that is supportive of neither collaboration nor employee morale. A study conducted by Accountemps in 2013 cited a breakdown in employee communications as the leading cause of poor employee morale, and it goes without saying that low morale equals low productivity and lack of commitment on the part of employees.[1]

When we combine these flaws it becomes apparent that we are *operating* our companies using an upside-down business model, misdirecting funds toward leadership rather than employee development, and applying a one-directional approach to communications from the top of the organization down, all with the expectation of maximizing productivity, profitability, and innovation.

In addition to these flaws, and in an effort to find restitution in quick-fix solutions to ongoing challenges with employees, many business executives have turned to changing *how* a business is operated, rather than focusing on *who* operates it. Our approach to managing business operations today is highly process and technology centric, not people centric, and in doing so we are losing the hearts, and more important, the minds of our employees. The majority of employees feel disempowered, disheartened, and discontent in their working environment, and it shows. A study of 142 countries conducted by Gallup in 2013 identified that only 13 percent of employees were truly engaged in their roles, meaning they were psychologically committed to their jobs and were most likely to make a positive contribution to their organization.[2]

Fortunately it's not all doom and gloom. Through our inability to achieve the desired levels of productivity and profitability while operating with these fundamental flaws and perceptions, a vision as to how organizations should be structured and operated in order to maximize productivity and profitability becomes much clearer. As Ralph Waldo Emerson once said, "Our strength grows out of our weaknesses."

Why Operational Excellence Is Not the Solution

In 1998, I was introduced to the concept of Lean at Ford Motor Company. At the time I had been invited as an employee of Magna International to participate in a supplier training and education event that was focused on introducing and integrating Lean practices into the supply chain. Ford was doing something that many other organizations were not, which was to invest in its suppliers and help them to recognize how they could improve their business in order to provide greater value to Ford, their customer. The intent was to create the proverbial "win-win" outcome: if you help me to reduce costs, then I will provide you with more business opportunities.

What I most remember about this event is not the concepts or ideas discussed, but the lack of engagement from the suppliers who were in attendance, most of whom were not in operations or supply chain management but found their way to the event from sales or business development. It became readily apparent through discussions over periodic breaks and dinner that the audience in attendance believed that, despite the event's intended purpose, it was a sales opportunity, not a proactive, engaging session to share ideas on how to improve Ford's—and in turn the attendees'—business. What was intended to improve business performance and profitability for Ford and its suppliers was less effective than desired because the right approach was used to engage the wrong audience. Herein lies the challenge with many business improvement initiatives and ideas. With the best of intentions a proven approach to business improvement is applied ineffectively, resulting in less-than-desirable outcomes, yet we blame the approach or methodology rather than the application.

Earlier in my corporate career, while working at a Fortune 500 company, human resources initiated an employee engagement survey that resulted in less-than-desirable scores. In order to improve the levels of employee engagement, one of the initiatives taken was to introduce an online employee rewards program, providing a mechanism for supervisors and managers to reward employees for a job well done. The belief presumably was that more employee recognition would equate to higher levels of engagement. Each manager and supervisor received a quantity of points each month, which they in turn had to award to their employees to recognize good performance. As the program progressed it became clear that supervisors were not awarding all of their allotted points to employees; moreover, employees were not interacting with their supervisors or managers any more than they had previously. The "solution" did not meet the needs of the employees, and it increased the workload of supervisors. Again, a proven approach to engagement was applied ineffectively, resulting in less-than-desirable outcomes.

This brings me to the concept of *operational excellence*, which has become the latest flavor of the month, an evolution of the historically popular term *manufacturing excellence* and designed with the intent of ensuring that initiatives and investments to improve productivity actually achieve their desired result. The phrase and accompanying framework provides an approach to improving operational performance to the point of achieving *excellence*. No small feat by any measure. The real question we must ask ourselves, however, is why "excellence?" Why would we invest in achieving excellence when, at least in some areas of the business, good enough is acceptable? I've found that many CEOs and senior business leaders I encounter seem to be enamored with the pursuit of operational excellence, which quickly becomes evident following a quick review of their vision statements and strategic objectives with phrases such as *achieve excellence* and *introduce operational excellence* peppered throughout. When I help an organization formulate its business strategy, invariably the phrase *operational excellence* creeps into our discussions at some point. When it does, I instinctively ask, "What does *operational excellence* mean?" The room typically falls silent as everyone struggles to formulate a clear and measurable definition of such a vague and spongy phrase. More specifically:

Who *defines* excellence?

How can we measure *excellence*?

What can we do to ensure a *return on our investment* in excellence?

Put bluntly, the term *operational excellence* is too vague. The sheer use of the word *excellence* suggests that this is something appealing, and in turn every organization should strive to achieve it, when in reality this is ludicrous, as the investment to pursue *excellence* most likely always outweighs any possible benefits to achieving it.

Consider some of the most significant and successful operational accomplishments of the twentieth century such as NASA putting the first man on the moon or Henry Ford improving upon the concept of mass production. In both of these instances, the concept of *operational excellence* was nonexistent, yet these seemingly impossible operational feats were accomplished. The pursuit of *Operational Excellence* suggests we are chasing an elusive outcome, not a reasonable target. Our focus needs instead to be on the specific and often dynamic operational inputs that achieve the desired outcome in performance measured in the form of productivity and profitability. Put in this manner it becomes apparent that we aren't seeking the attainment of excellence, but rather we are seeking to be effective.

When we shift from the vague, and seemingly unreasonable, target of achieving excellence to instead being effective, the focus areas become much clearer. An operation of any size or magnitude after all is only as effective as the people that support it, both internally and externally. Achieving operational effectiveness in turn requires that we design a structured approach to capitalizing on external resource collaboration, engage employees to continuously improve business processes, and sustain an injection of both internal and open sources of innovation. To capitalize on any of these three areas in turn requires clarity (to those involved both internally and externally) as to *the reason for the improvement* (what's in it for me), *the urgency for implementing and sustaining the improvements* (why should I treat this as a priority), *and how it is supported by a collective vision* (how will this help us). (See Figure 1.1.)

FIGURE 1.1 Operational Effectiveness

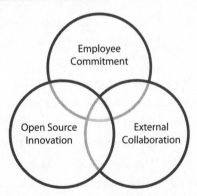

Employee commitment + External collaboration without Innovation = *a lack of fresh ideas*
External collaboration + Innovation without Employee commitment = *an inability to implement change*
Open source innovation + Employee commitment without External collaboration = *lack of new ideas and best practices*

From my experience in working with companies from around the globe, I have found that the most significant attributes of any operationally effective company are as follows:

- Their vision is not just a statement, but a guide from which decisions are made.
- Their leadership operates as a single collaborative unit, demonstrating the desired behaviors and attributes of the organization.
- Unionized or otherwise, the decision-making atmosphere is one of collaboration and action, not command and control.
- Customer value is at the forefront of all decisions surrounding business operations. If the customer won't find benefit, it is unlikely to happen.
- Employees identify, design, and initiate improvements to business processes, not a separate department or function within the company.
- Employee decision-making autonomy is more important than satisfying procedural requirements.
- Suppliers, contractors, and affiliates are considered strategic partners and are leveraged for innovative ideas and opportunities.
- Technology selection and integration is done collaboratively across the business, with employees being the predominant stakeholders.
- Everyone understands how his or her efforts contribute to the customer and ultimately profitability for the company.

For the complete list of the attributes and measures of operationally effective companies as well as dozens of other resources to empower your operation, visit www.operationalempowerment.com.

As I alluded to earlier, the fundamental flaws we have built our businesses upon have in turn led us down the path of seeking a "quick fix" to improve productivity and profitability. Operational excellence is the latest trend in a long list of initiatives that promises rapid and effective solutions; however, we are ignoring reality if we believe that the pursuit of excellence will yield our desired results. It is only through the identification of methods to be operationally effective that we can clearly define what success looks like and exactly how we can achieve it.

The Operational Disconnect

CEOs, senior executives, and even executive directors often make decisions based on what they have been told, not what has been verified as valid and valuable information. Once while serving on a board of directors of a not-for-profit association, we had a member who became highly agitated and disgruntled with the direction of the association. The executive director provided recommendations to the board on how we should respond to the allegations and claims made by the member; however, when we asked the executive director where he attained his information, he admitted that it was compiled from discussions with one of his senior staff members. That's right—not once had the executive director attempted to reach out and speak directly with the disgruntled member or seek input or validation from other association members as to the relevance of the feedback. The information the executive director was ready to act upon was unqualified and based on the perspectives of one individual who was removed from the situation. Herein lies another significant contributor to poor decisions in improving operational performance today. Our desire for a quick fix often leads us to make hasty decisions based on unqualified information.

CEOs, business owners, and executives consistently make decisions based on a combination of experience and both qualified and unqualified information. Qualified information is that which is relevant, important, and validated for our use. Information that flows from trade associations, peer networks, and even business consultants is often qualified. Unqualified information is that which is often from a single source, contains opinion and conjecture, supports personal agendas, or is initiated to cause a reaction.

You may recall the game of telephone, often played by children, where a message is crafted and then passed around a circle, being transferred from child to child. The result often is that the message that reaches the last child in the circle is significantly different from the message that was originally crafted. Each child acts as a filter to the information, creating slight modifications to the message's intent as it is passed along. This type of filtering is exactly what happens across organizations as messages from employees on the front lines get transferred to those in executive positions. The more managers that exist between the employees and the CEO, the greater the chance that information will be filtered based on the personal agendas, priorities, and objectives of managers. In turn information that reaches the executive suite is unqualified. In Figure 1.2 I identify how these filters exist and their influence on information.

Examples of unqualified information resulting in poor decision making in business are everywhere. A recent report on CNBC identified how an attempt by McDonald's to develop an online financial planning tool for employees actually resulted in a clear demonstration of how impossible it is for employees to survive financially solely on the wages McDonald's provides.[3]

Here is the kicker. It's through information, both qualified and unqualified, that upper management makes decisions and takes action, allocating funds and selecting resources to overcome operational challenges and improve business performance. The outcome is often significant financial investments and shifts in business focus and direction that *do not* target the root cause of the real challenges the business faces.

I call this this phenomenon the *operational disconnect*, as demonstrated in Figure 1.2.

FIGURE 1.2 Operational Disconnect

Senior Leadership

Operational Disconnect

Employees

Earlier I touched upon my employment at a Fortune 500 company, a business that had several very powerful unions amid its operation. As an organization, it was struggling to improve its operational effectiveness. When speaking with frontline staff, the number one comment I heard was that the CEO *used to* visit the shop floor to discuss employee challenges and provide feedback about the business. Through these actions, employees were left feeling that the CEO understood what they were dealing with on a daily basis, and they in turn felt that he was taking the right actions to move the company forward. Somewhere along the line, the CEO ceased this level of interaction and replaced it with quarterly town hall meetings. The lack of focus and engagement within the business could be measured back to the point at which the face-to-face interaction between the lowest and highest levels of the organization ceased. Though his intention had been to focus more on the business, the CEO had inadvertently shunned his employees, resulting in a reduction in both employee engagement and productivity.

To further demonstrate the operational disconnect and its impact on operational performance, let's consider a very common challenge of data capture and reporting. In every business, upper management requires data to understand business performance, but often this data needs to be collected and manipulated in order to provide the desired information. Somewhere along the line an error is often spotted in existing reports, or possibly new information is deemed unattainable based on existing system protocols and functionality. What's the outcome? If the reports are required by senior management or the board, a significant investment will be made to attain the correct data, and most likely in this example the result will be a new enterprise resource planning (ERP) program. How does this come about? After direction comes from senior management to "fix the problem," the IT department will make some calls; then some individuals in very fine suits will present their software solution that will often do everything but shampoo the carpets, and presto—new software implementation. Now let me ask you, during this process did anyone ever confer with the frontline staff to understand what system capabilities and reporting they need to do their job more effectively? Not likely. How about engaging end users of the software in reviewing and providing feedback on various features or system options? Not likely. This example may seem unwarranted, but in my experience technology selection and integration is one of the most prominent and detrimental influences today on productivity, and the example I provided above on how the solution is selected and integrated is all too common among North American businesses. As I mentioned earlier, we are operating with a significant disconnect between what shareholders, owners, and senior management believe will improve productivity and what those actually doing the tasks need to improve productivity.

The key to overcoming the operational disconnect is to be able to minimize the gap between actual operational needs and senior management's interpretation of those needs.

Earlier last year I was having lunch with the director of finance for a North American cement manufacturer. During our discussions he confided to me his frustration with a recent situation where senior executives had acted on unqualified information, making decisions and taking actions that were misguided and a complete waste of time for the business. The issue had initially arisen when an executive was advised that accounts receivable had been extending beyond 30 days for some time. The first level of investigation was finance, who suggested that the challenge was in the ability to rapidly process invoices due to submission delays from vendors. The problem was then directed to purchasing to "fix the vendor issue." Through the director's investigation it became clear that the "vendor issue" was actually delays caused by the business operations (the group responsible to receive vendor products and produce cement), as they were not signing for any goods received, causing finance to reject receipts and forcing vendors to spend weeks attempting to contact the operations department to request signatures that would allow them to be paid for goods already delivered.

Ultimately communication gaps exist across all levels of an organization, as well as between the business and its customers, suppliers, and affiliates. Overcoming the operational disconnect through multifaceted communications is the only means by which to engage employees, suppliers, and customers in order to create a business of perpetual profits and long-term sustainability.

The Operational Imperative: Why Is Now the Right Time?

The global marketplace is no longer something to consider becoming a part of; it's here, and along with it is competition that can do what you do faster, smarter, and often cheaper. To survive in today's economy, CEOs, business owners, executives, and directors have to come to grips with the urgent need to empower their operation in order to stand apart from their competition.

Procter & Gamble is a great example of an organization that recognizes the need to improve its operational performance in order to stay ahead of its competition. CEO A. G. Lafley was largely responsible for the initial introduction at Procter & Gamble of an open innovation model, aptly titled Connect + Develop.[4] This approach to innovation attracts and connects with entrepreneurs, suppliers, inventors, and other outside resources to find solutions to improve its products or services. P&G was ahead of its competition when it introduced this model, which it continues to improve and enhance today.

Companies that understand the operational imperative readily acknowledge their weaknesses relative to delivering on customer commitments while maximizing company profitability and embracing rapid and dramatic change in order to drive sustained improvements. They recognize that customer attraction and retention is the direct result of the combination of both great marketing *and* great execution. They understand the importance of delivering on their strategy, and they demonstrate this ability consistently, despite the various obstacles that present themselves along the journey. They also recognize that success in operational execution is consistently achieved when they have stronger relationships and interdependencies between their employees, suppliers, and customers.

2

Operational Building Blocks: A Foundation for Growth and Profitability

A Lagging Foundation Leads to Lost Opportunity

Every structure requires a solid foundation. The foundation of a skyscraper can be up to 150 feet in depth, determined by assessing the height and structure of the building, the soil conditions, and of course the lateral forces that will be placed on the structure. By taking a proactive approach to designing, planning, and forming a foundation built to withstand the test of time, a skyscraper is assured of standing tall despite the forces it may encounter for decades, if not centuries, to come. We also know from history that if the foundation is weak, it is not a matter of *if* the skyscraper will crumble, but *when*.

We've learned through time that this same proactive approach yields the strongest and most enduring companies. Despite being behind schedule and well over the original estimated budget, Richard Branson continues his quest to fly people to the moon. His team continues to proactively assess, prepare for, and plan the best technologies, materials, and designs that will achieve this outcome. Creating a solid foundation on which to fly people to the moon may seem illogical based on the risks involved, but I would suggest to you that it is sound business sense, something that Mr. Branson is well known and widely recognized for.

Contrast this tested and proven approach to building a solid foundation for a business against the structure and foundation within most company operations today, and you will find less of a proactive approach and more of a reactive approach. Investments in equipment, technology, and resources are often made well after customer demands (both internally and externally) are present. Consider your own business operation: Did you put the entire operational structure in place prior to the very first customer order, or did you grow and evolve the structure in support of increasing customer demand? My guess is the later.

Having spent much of his career as a plant manager and now as vice president of operations, a close friend and colleague Dale Schnurr admits that a good portion of his time is spent on identifying the basic foundational needs of the operation, then influencing the CEO and often his team as to why the investment is necessary. New equipment, more resources, training, and improvements in technology are often lagging in contrast to demand of both internal and external customers, as well as what the market has to offer.

We are structuring the foundation of our business operations in a reactive or lagging fashion, growing and improving them in accordance with business demands long after the demand has been well established.

Figure 2.1 shows a reactive approach to managing an operational foundation.

FIGURE 2.1 Reactive Operational Structure

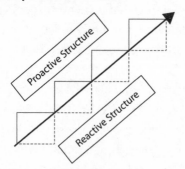

During a recent meeting with the owner of a wood furniture manu-facturer, it became apparent that business was booming! When I asked the CEO about the stability of orders, he was almost embarrassed to admit that the company was several weeks behind on orders. Its lead time had crept considerably higher than average, and even higher than the typical backlog the company experienced during peak seasons. As we discussed his order backlog, it became readily apparent that several key issues had led to this rather unusual situation:

1. The company was in its peak season, where a multiweek backlog was historically the norm.
2. It had been unsuccessful in convincing the majority of its employ-ees to work overtime.
3. The historic seasonal demand trends had never warranted initiat-ing a second shift.
4. Complexity in the manufacturing process resulted in a learning curve of several months.
5. The majority of employees specialized in only one area of the oper-ation with very little cross-training.

The company's response to this unusual spike in demand was to accept whatever overtime employees would provide, as well as hiring some temporary staff for simple tasks. It applied a lagging approach (overtime, increased inventory levels) on a micro scale to deal with its immense backlog. As a result of predictable seasonal trends that impacted demand, it was not considering responding on a macro level (hiring additional permanent staff, initiating a second shift). The foun-dation of its operation was built to handle a fixed volume of work, and its response to an increase in volume lagged the capacity requirements.

A lagging response to forming a solid operational foundation may seem like a logical approach when you consider the costs and risks associated with building a foundation proactively. There are few com-panies that actually feel comfortable investing in acquiring equipment and new technology, hiring highly skilled employees, and developing the skills of the existing workforce without first having long-term and predictable stability in customer demand. Unfortunately, however, a lagging approach to an operational foundation results in several business demonetizing challenges:

- Extended delivery and wait times for customers, which is destructive to sustaining customer demand.
- High volumes of work thrust upon a fixed employee base, increasing demands on employees and diminishing morale.
- An increased risk of defective material and poor service delivery as increased volumes tap the capacity of existing capabilities.

Each of these challenges is detrimental to the long-term business success, profitability, and viability of any company. On the surface it would seem logical to form a sufficient foundation for any operation, one that is built to withstand predicted and potential volume and capacity challenges. Logical in theory, that is—but name me a CEO, business owner, or investor who will invest capital when the financial returns are clearly lagging the investment and have no guarantee or promise of being realized. We instead operate in a lagging fashion without a clear understanding as to the *cost of lost opportunities.*

I would surmise that for most (if not all) of you reading this that your operational foundation is already in place, fully functional . . . and lagging as described above. Fortunately, I will tell you that there is hope. If a complete restructure of your operations is not entirely feasible, or necessary, reinforcing its long-term stability is quite possible if you address the five key components of an operationally effective business.

Operational Component #1: Balancing Pie in the Sky with a Dose of Reality

In the strategy work I do with my clients, I often find it's the individuals who are functioning in the day-to-day business operations that have the greatest challenge in becoming engaged in forming the company's vision. I've studied well over two dozen separate businesses and found repeatedly that for every creative idea that is generated to identify what

the future vision of the organization should be, there are several opposing issues, concerns, or challenges that an operational leader such as a
COO, vice president of operations, or plant manager can surmise. The
reason? They have been at the bleeding edge of making the company
operations what they are today, attempting to operate efficiently while
managing with a lagging foundation. In essence, I've found that they
are unable to easily agree to forming a proactive vision when all they've
experienced is a reactive and difficult journey to reach current (and
likely unsatisfactory) levels of performance.

The challenge in formulating a powerful and meaningful vision is in
creating a realization of the necessary actions and investments to ensure
it is achieved. In a vision session when creative juices are flowing, it's
easy to get carried away and dream big, but when faced with the realization that investments in people, equipment, or technology are necessary
to achieve the vision, suddenly momentum slows and energy wanes.

A longstanding client of mine, Larsen and Shaw Limited, has a
very clear and powerful vision. The company is known as "The Hinge
People." As you might surmise, it manufactures and sells hinges, from
residential hinges to large commercial hinges for construction, automotive purposes, and heavy equipment. While revisiting the company's
strategy a couple of years ago, we spent some time reconsidering its
vision. Hinges were still its main product line, but it had expanded into
other markets offering a broader array of products and services that had
offered increasing value to its customers. After careful consideration, we
came up with a slightly revised but equally powerful vision, and today
the company is "The Hinge People+." The addition of the "+" symbol
signifies the additional value it offers its customers, all of which still falls
under providing the greatest service and value relative to hinge manufacturers in the market.

What was most powerful about this exercise was how we came to the
conclusion of the revised vision statement. Prior to the session, I had
met and spoken with all of the company's frontline leadership staff, the
majority of whom were functioning under the umbrella of operations. At
the initial stages of the visioning session I presented to the senior management team some of the feedback I had received to the questions asked.

The specific employee feedback we focused on was in response to the following questions:

1. What are the strengths of Larsen and Shaw today as you see them?
2. What are the challenges and/or opportunities that are facing Larsen and Shaw today?
3. What are the three things you would change at Larsen and Shaw given your role if there were no limitations?

It was through engagement of the operational frontline leadership that we were able to ensure that the vision remained grounded in the current direction and ambitions of the organization and remained a meaningful and powerful statement. Notice the clarity in Larsen and Shaw's vision of "The Hinge People+." This is a statement that every single employee, supplier, and customer can understand, connect with, and support.

Equally important is the fact that this vision provides the basis upon which decisions can be made. Investments in technology, equipment, or venturing into new product lines can easily be considered relative to whether they support or hinder the company vision.

Consider the play on words that can be derived from this vision statement and how it supports Larsen and Shaw's decision making.

1. "*The*" Hinge People: The first and most recognized choice for hinge needs.
2. The "*Hinge*" People: Representing all things that are hinge related in its market, from design to manufacturer to distribution.
3. The Hinge "*People*": A clear focus on the further development and nurturing of its people, as its people are truly behind the business and its success.

Any decisions that support, enhance, or capitalize on any or all of these three scenarios are instinctively in line with Larsen and Shaw's vision and can easily be understood and thereby supported by employees, suppliers, and contractors due to the vision's simplicity and clarity.

The most valuable visions then are those that:

- Include input from frontline employees and leaders
- Are considered carefully by a cross-functional group based on the current opportunities and challenges faced by the business
- Do not significantly shift or change each time the vision is considered
- Will provide the basis for quality decisions around investment and focus for the company
- Can be clearly understood and explained by each and every employee working within the organization
- Can be clearly understood by customers, suppliers, and the general public

In essence a vision is a statement that supports delivering significant value to existing and prospective customers both today and in future years. Through an engaging approach to vision formulation and careful consideration of input from all work groups, particularly operations, the vision will remain based in the reality and commitment to incorporating the necessary structure and foundation to deliver that value.

Operational Component #2: Community over Culture

Studies of organizational culture date back decades, with some of the most recognized work done by Gerard Hendrik Hofstede. Hofstede formulated a cultural dimensions theory to assess, differentiate, and understand various organizational cultures. He hypothesized that there are national and regional cultural groups that influence behavior of societies and organizations. Within each organizational culture are subcultures, a component of the region, demographics, and varying social and ethnical backgrounds of those employees who work within the organization.[1] Gerard and scores of other psychologists who have followed his lead have invested a tremendous amount of effort on studying, understanding, and improving upon organizational culture, yet a weak organizational culture remains one of the greatest risks to sustaining business performance.[2]

Before launching my consulting business, my career spanned eight companies in seven industries over a seventeen-year period. During this time I was involved in an organization-wide cultural assessment at least four separate times. These assessments came in various forms, but were most recognized as an employee engagement survey. For each of these assessments, my experience has been that it fell upon members of leadership to change how they interacted, managed, and engaged with employees.

This perception is wrong. In my experience, we are looking at cultural engagement in an entirely wrong manner, mostly on account of the foundational flaws I outline in Chapter 3.

Employees simply want to be involved and feel like they belong. It's been proven in a dozen different ways that employees who feel involved, recognized, and appreciated are more productive.[3] Business leaders create these environments not through a focus on manipulating the organizational culture, or a singular focus on changing how we lead, but instead through the formation of communities.

Consider for a moment what most people do when they have spare time. They invest their time in interacting with other people, be it at a water cooler, sports club, or hockey arena, or online using social media. We are a culture that desires human interaction, plain and simple. We are naturally drawn to those with similar interests, those who possess answers we seek, and those groups that offer support and nurturing. This is why organizations such as the Rotary Club, professional associations, and even fitness clubs have existed for so long, and will continue to exist moving forward albeit in a different form than we are accustomed to today.

If we consider the characteristics of these various communities, we uncover ideas that support the formation of a powerful, attractive, and value-added community, namely:

- They are built around individuals who possess similar interests, ideas, and desires.
- Collectively they offer opportunities, information, and ideas that support our desired growth.
- We can solicit and offer advice, providing fulfillment and a sense of self-worth.

- There are few rules, and the rules or guidelines that do exist are frequently adjusted to meet the needs of members.
- There are opportunities to work in small groups or large groups, depending on individual preferences.
- Information is available for consumption, but not forced or mandated.
- Opportunities to further one's status are often voluntary and not necessary.

For more information on the components of and how to design your own powerful corporate community, as well as dozens of other resources, visit www.operationalempowerment.com.

I'm not suggesting that we retool how we operate in business—at least not entirely. What I am suggesting is that if we form operational communities of like-minded individuals, we dramatically increase the likelihood of retaining, entertaining, and engaging the very employees, suppliers, and contractors who support operations (Figure 2.2).

FIGURE 2.2 Operational Community

People are drawn to and participate in communities that they deem offer them value. They show up on time, participate actively, and provide support and encouragement to others. This is the foundation of an empowered operation. You can't force a square peg into a round hole, but if you create a large enough hole and let others know about it, there will be plenty of pegs, square, round, and triangular, that will fit.

Caframo Limited is a great example of an organization that has an operational community. When you pass through the facility, regardless of the time of day, you will always receive several smiles, some cheerful "hellos," and even a question about what help you might require. As a major employer in a small community, Caframo's president, Tony Solecki, along with his vice president of operations and his plant manager, has always focused on building a strong community. Employees know and interact with one another and often live in the same community; hence their interests are aligned around their desire to work in the town they love, stay connected with others in the community, and participate in meaningful work that contains both variety and challenge.

At Caframo, employees who desire the opportunity to grow in their career are encouraged to speak up; there are numerous cross-functional job rotations that allow employees who desire variety in their work to experience other positions, or employees may choose a stable repetitive task if that is their preference. Each day begins and ends with a small group huddle, during which all employees discuss the projects for the day, upcoming changes to the schedule, parts shortages, and any other information that is pertinent to ensuring they are successful. In addition to frequent intercompany dialogue, employees are encouraged to participate in various activities including a chili cook-off, several raffles throughout the year, and an annual group Walk for Cancer. During these events there is no segregation between those working on the shop floor and those in the office.

Tony has been highly successful at building a community of like-minded and supportive employees, and employee retention, product quality, and positive employee morale all support the continued growth and progression of the business. Focus on building a stronger community where employees want to work, and you will worry less about engaging those who don't want to work.

Operational Component #3: Getting the "How" Right

Effective outcomes—business, personal, or even professional—are a result of doing the right things at the right time, with the three choice words being:

1. Doing—taking action toward the achievement of desired outcomes.
2. Things—activities, steps, practices that will yield a valuable outcome.
3. Time—a period or moment in which you are solely focused on achieving that outcome.

Successful outcomes, be they initiatives, projects, or investments, in any business then require an alignment across all these elements. For example, if we do the wrong things at the wrong time, we will not achieve the outcomes we desire. When Netflix decided to split its streaming and DVD business into two separate companies, Netflix and Quickster, it was met with outrage from longstanding customers who valued the simplicity of Netflix's former business model, which allowed them a "one-stop shop" opportunity for all of their media needs. Amid the public outcry, Netflix quickly rescinded its decision, and CEO Reed Hastings released a statement, saying, "Consumers value the simplicity Netflix has always offered and we respect that. There is a difference between moving quickly—which Netflix has done very well for years—and moving too fast, which is what we did in this case."[4] Clearly Netflix's model was working extremely well for customers, hence any change that was intended to meet internal stakeholder needs (splitting into two separate entities) was the wrong decision, and the fact that the company made a hasty announcement without first entertaining the idea among its many supporters made it the wrong time to make the decision.

Suppose, however, that we make the right decision at the wrong time? RIM's BlackBerry was once the dominant player in mobile technology, with the highly popular QWERTY keyboard remaining a favorite of mobile users for nearly a decade. Beginning in 2010, however, continued advances in Apple and Samsung products began to take a foothold, slowly diminishing RIM's market share. In retrospect it's easy to ascertain that the delayed decision to move to more consumer desirable touch-screen technology, and a failure to successfully launch into the tablet market are the contributing factors that resulted in the rapid decline of RIM's brand, reputation, and revenue. RIM's move to introduce touch-screen capability in its Z10 mobile technology, in conjunction with refocusing on narrowing its technology focus, ultimately slowed the rapid decline. Time will tell if this move was made fast enough to save the company from going bankrupt. RIM did make the right decision in moving into competitive technology and releasing its belief that the once desirable QWERTY keyboard would retain its dominance at a time when consumers were demanding touch screen, but the decision was made too late. This was the right decision at the wrong time.

As a practitioner and teacher of Lean for nearly two decades, one of the most powerful lessons I've adopted is that Lean offers a constant reminder that we must focus our effort (the doing) on the right things (activities, tasks, practices) at the right time (on time and in the most efficient sequence) *in order to add value for our customers.* To this end, striving to continuously deliver value to customers requires that we first understand:

1. What we should be doing (the vision).
2. Who will be involved (the operational community).
3. How we will add value (the processes, activities, and steps that drive value).

Delivering value in turn then results from assessing the right vision (what the customer will value), the right resources (who and what we will need to build and deliver the value), and lastly the optimum approach or work flow (how to deliver the value in the most effective and efficient way possible to maximize profits). (See Figure 2.3.)

FIGURE 2.3 How We Create Customer Value

However simplistic this may seem, my experience is that it is this third element, the *how*, that, although seemingly the most straightforward to identify and put into practice, presents us with the greatest challenge to maximizing operational performance and effectiveness. Consider, for example, which department is predominantly the most aligned with and closest to the customer. For most businesses, this would be anyone who falls under the umbrella of sales and marketing. Now consider the department that is often furthest removed from the sales and marketing team: production and operations. Which of these two groups has to do the right things at the right time to maximize value to the customer? Production and operations. Does this seem right to you?.

Through the work I've done with clients I've found that there are five steps for effectively achieving the *how*, namely:

1. Understand what the customer (internally and externally) values.
2. Initiate cross-functional collaboration to ascertain the most effective and efficient approach to delivering the value.
3. Agreement on how time should be focused and invested (focus on value-added activities).
4. Create clarity to ensure that even the most complex steps and actions are understood.

5. Instill congruence surrounding when actions are necessary to maximize value to the customer.

For more ideas on how to create customer value for your organization, as well as dozens of other resources to empower your operation, visit www.operationalempowerment.com.

Let's look at the *how* in action. Before an airplane can take off, the pilots spend considerable time obtaining and analyzing information to ensure that they can achieve their vision (reach their destination on time), using the support of their operational community (the ground crew, stewardesses, air traffic control). Before a plane even departs, the flight crew completes their preflight checks, during which they review their flight plan, look at wind speed and weather, and consider the weight of their airplane in order to best balance their load. Preflight checks are formed through addressing the *how*:

1. Customers want to arrive on time.
2. Pilots, flight crew, and ground crews must work collaboratively to ensure on-time departure and arrival.
3. Predetermined time estimations must be met to ensure on-time departure and arrival.
4. Extensive training, detailed procedures, and checks ensure that everyone understands his or her role.
5. Activities are sequenced in the most efficient and effective means to ensure on-time departure and arrival.

The consistency with which top-performing airlines such as Southwest, Delta, and Air Canada ensure these steps are met provides us (the customers) with a higher than average safe and on-time arrival at our desired destination when you compare it to other forms of travel such as by automobile, train, or boat.

Now consider a situation where the five steps to achieving the *how* are not enacted correctly. In 1999, the Mars Climate Orbiter burned up after coming within 37 miles of the Martian surface, 16 miles closer to the surface than it was ever supposed to be. An investigation after the incident found that engineers failed to catch and convert metric measurements in a component of thruster software to imperial units in order to ensure the software functioned correctly with other software, allowing full control over the orbiter's thrusters. The mistake was not found until the investigation of the crash, despite the engineers receiving several warning signs that something was amiss, including additional adjustments to thrust that could not be explained as well as distance and direction calculations that were not in alignment with the flight plan. In this circumstance, the failure to achieve the desired vision (place the satellite safely into the Martian orbit), was not achieved as a result of failures in level two, four, and five of the *how* process; more specifically:

1. Cross-functional collaboration was not sufficient enough to catch the difference in measurement units.
2. There was insufficient clarity relative to how the software was to function to support thrust.
3. Engineers failed to take action when they found that additional actions and time were necessary to keep the orbiter on the correct path.

The only way to ensure that we are doing the right things at the right time is to ensure that the five steps to achieving the *how* have been addressed. In fact, our inability to consistently achieve this objective is the very reason practices such as Lean, Six Sigma, and Business Process Redesign have gained in popularity as tools for improving business performance. They address the *how* and yield new insights into ways to deliver greater value in the fastest, most cost-effective means possible.

In order to achieve the organization's vision utilizing the operational community, all CEOs, presidents, and executives of today's companies must ascertain *how to best govern the investment of time to yield the maximum value for our customers, shareholders, and employees.* Fundamentally, how employees invest time will determine whether the business grows, sustains, or diminishes. Invested wisely, time can yield significant value to the customer in record time with little effort, but if invested poorly, time can result in very little value at a substantial cost, and it's this latter outcome that is the nemesis of a successful, thriving operation (Figure 2.4).

FIGURE 2.4 Value Time to Market

The criticality and urgency of ensuring that we do things in the most efficient and effective means possible can be easily determined if we look at the balance sheet and ask, "What percentage of our costs are invested in salaries, wages, and benefits for our employees?" Any investment that doesn't yield a significant return is waste, and having people do the wrong things at the wrong time, or spend their time battling internal processes or work groups in order to achieve their own desired outcomes, is a sunk investment.

Operational Component #4: The Right Tools for the Job

Doing the right things in a timely fashion is a result of having the right tools for the job. One of the most respected leaders that I ever worked for was Bob Johnson. Bob was the plant manager for a large automotive company where I worked for several years, and I admired the way he interacted with his people. Despite the difficulties in the automotive market at the time, Bob always asked employees at his plant what they needed to be more efficient at their roles, and then despite budget constraints and other challenges, Bob would find ways to provide these tools. Bob also practiced what he preached. Although cell phones were quite common during Bob's tenure, I recall that rarely did you find him carrying one, at a time when other managers were addicted to the rapid access to e-mail and telephone. On one such occasion I was at an off-site facility with Bob for a corporate meeting. Throughout the day during breaks and lunch, Bob spent time interacting with the other managers and employees to obtain their thoughts, concerns, and ideas for improving the operation. I wondered how Bob ever found the time to answer his messages, recognizing that he was in a role that demanded far more attention and time than my role did. As a leader of 238 employees in a unionized environment under a corporate umbrella of similar business units, you can imagine that Bob was under considerable pressure both internally and corporately. Following the meeting, I approached Bob and asked if we could meet to speak the following day, to which Bob replied that although he had to get home for dinner, I could call him on his cell phone shortly to chat if it was urgent.

Surprised, I replied, "Bob, I didn't think you used your cell phone!"

"Of course," he responded, "but I make all of my return calls on my drive home; I find it's less distracting than during my day, and of course if someone needs me so urgently that they can't wait until the end of the day, they can find ways to reach me." Profound, I thought—despite the accessibility and convenience cell phones provided us, Bob had found a way to make the technology work for him and instead focus his attention on collaborating within the community that he was building.

Having worked with executives from high-performing organizations from around the world, I've found that the companies that have the most effective operations are those that have placed considerable investment and time into understanding what it is their employees require to rapidly deliver value to their customers. They recognize that to achieve the *how* they need to first understand what it is that will support their people so they are both efficient in what they do and effective at doing it, and they place a priority on investing not in the solutions that they deem necessary but in resources that their employees deem necessary.

Tools for the purposes of delivering customer value can be in the form of technology, as I mentioned earlier, but technology has had such a poor influence on operations today that I have saved it as a separate discussion point. Therefore, aside from technology, ensuring that we do the right things at the right time is a result of having the right work-space, the right equipment, the right tools, and sufficient knowledge and expertise, all in a collaborative environment. These resources in turn become the tools to support doing the right things at the right time, in order to effectively achieve the organizational vision.

I spent time earlier in my career working at Bellwyck Packaging, a supplier of premium packaging to the pharmaceutical and cosmetic industry. We shipped our completed premium boxes to customers in much larger corrugated boxes. During my time with the company the complexity and breadth of our product line had grown significantly, meaning that the varied sizes and shapes of the premium packaging required that we continue to expand the sizes and shape of the corrugated boxes we purchased. You can imagine then that as the number of sizes and styles of corrugated boxes, a purchased product, grew in both size and volume, so too did our inventory. It became the nightmare of all nightmares when completing annual physical inventories, and a decision was made to consider purchasing our own corrugated box–making machine. After assessing several options and weighing the costs versus benefits, we sourced and installed a machine that had the capacity to exceed our volume demands. Through proper training and streamlining of our internal processes, we were easily able to integrate the box maker, which allowed us several expected benefits (reduced inventory levels, increased flexibility in corrugated box sizes), as well as several unexpected benefits (the shift to producing corrugated boxes just in time, and the opportunity to outsource additional corrugated box making capacity to other companies as a potential revenue stream).

Fortunately, the owner of the company was eager to support decisions that allowed employees and the company the opportunity to continue to do the right things at the right time, all while continuously improving company efficiency and capability. He was intently focused on a proactive approach to growth, rather than a reactive approach.

It's unreasonable to think that employees can be efficient if they don't possess the right space, layout, equipment, tools, and resources to complete their jobs efficiently. Contrary to what you might believe, companies that do not provide sufficient tools and resources to their employees are not just those that lack the necessary funds to invest. I've worked with some high-growth and highly profitable companies where, despite the availability of cash and resources, their predominant focus resides in investing in marketing and sales growth, rather than investing in the operations that support their growth.

Providing the right tools then, as you can tell, comes down to three fundamental needs:

1. **Priority.** Is there a clear understanding of what is required to oper-ate efficiently, and is priority placed on ensuring the necessary tools, equipment, and resources are in place?
2. **Budget.** Is sufficient budget set aside to support the purchase and integration of the necessary tools and resources to support efficient operations?
3. **Time.** Has sufficient time been invested working with the right people in order to research, test, source, and integrate the most effective tools and resources to support operational effectiveness?

A couple of years ago I decided to finish our basement. I spent some time nailing together two-by-fours into a formation that I thought somewhat resembled a wall. After much coaxing and cajoling, I con-vinced a close friend, Jeremy, a contractor by trade, to come over and help me. My wife was astounded at the progress we had made after a single afternoon, and so was I. Our progress obviously was a result of Jeremy's knowledge of what to do and when to do it, but it was also a component of having the right tools and equipment. "Where's your tool belt?" he would ask. "Do you know how much time you can save if you have the right tools at your fingertips?" The list of recommendations went on, including suggestions for a better ladder, a better hammer, and even a better miter saw. Each time Jeremy made a recommendation, he spent the time showing me his tools and how their superiority to mine helped to get the job done faster and to a higher standard than what I could accomplish on my own.

The right tools can make all the difference when it comes to being effective at what we are doing, and who better to tell you what they need than your employees. I've never met an employee, either in my corporate career or as a consultant, that didn't have numerous ideas about the different tools that would make his or her job faster, easier, and more predictable. The challenge is collecting, validating, and acting on these suggestions. In Chapter 1, I spoke of our continued desire to manage using a hierarchy that is decades old and how this in turn promotes a top-down style of management. This top-down approach results in employees' ideas being filtered several times before they ever make it to the ears of those who have the power to make an investment. The larger the organization, the less likely it is that employees will have the tools they need to be effective, as the company hierarchy will be more structured and predominant. Let's be honest; supervisors or managers are only going to take an idea for investment in new tools or equipment to their boss if it is something that they understand, agree with, and support. In essence it must be logical to the supervisor or manager if he or she is going to escalate the idea to those who make the final investment decision. This limits the number of employee ideas that are acted upon, and as employees' ideas fall upon deaf ears, the number and quality of ideas diminish, resulting in a downward spiral of diminishing productivity and employee morale.

Operational Component #5: Out of the Box Technology Hinders Out of the Box Thinking

The last building block, the one that can make or break a business even before it is integrated, is technology. I've never met anyone in business that doesn't believe that technology can improve operational performance, maximize data availability and accuracy, and generally improve the efficiency of operations; and to an extent they are correct. Unfortunately, in my experience, however, technology is the one tool that we believe will yield greater value than what we actually experience. I'm still undecided as to whether this is an outcome of great marketing and selling on the part of technology companies, or if our desire to identify and introduce the fastest solution to improve our operational effectiveness is the culprit. My instincts tell me that it's a combination of both of these factors, with the former capitalizing on the later. Regardless, technology is a tool, not a guarantee of a result.

I should take a moment to clarify that for the purposes of our discussion in this chapter, when I refer to technology I'm referring to software that supports data capture and reporting, such as enterprise resource planning (ERP) and warehouse management systems (WMS), as it is a common platform for all business operations of today, whether you are in manufacturing, distribution, or even in association management. Technology related to operating equipment would be too broad for our discussions here.

In my first job at Magna International, I worked as a logistics scheduler alongside a small team of other college graduates coordinating the movement of nearly 160 loads of outbound freight each day. Fundamentally, the job involved coordinating the movement of outbound freight based on material handler availability and driver arrival and departure times. Tactically, we provided the necessary documents to drivers for shipment of the loads, followed by logging each load into the online system transmitting ASNs (advance ship notices). Although there was some variety (drivers arriving late, last-minute changes in load configurations, or frustrated material handlers who enjoyed razzing the logistics coordinators), invariably the job was quite routine, and I recall thinking two distinct thoughts at the time: *I'm not using any of the skills that I just spent three years learning in college*, and *They're actually going to pay me money to do this?*

After progressing from logistics into production planning at Magna over the next few years, I left to pursue a career in a large international electronics firm with the intent of taking a different direction in my career. What I found once I arrived at this new organization was that its technology and tools were drastically different from those at Magna. The Magna facility where I worked had a very robust IT department, including several individuals who could write code. What this meant was that all of the systems and technology that we used to gather, report, and manipulate data were developed by the internal employee team. In the remote chance an outside software solution was required, it was typically highly customized by the IT team in order to allow for seamless integration with the other software already in place. This was not a compilation of various software solutions each having its own feel and functionality, but a seamless symphony of technology all housed under a single operating system. In retrospect, it was heaven.

As an employee at Magna, I relied heavily on the system to collect and report data, allowing me to plan capacity and inventory quickly and accurately. I specifically recall walking down the hall to see John, a programmer who worked on the same floor, to tell him exactly what I needed to accomplish. Within days John would call me back to his office to show me what he had created, and after a few tweaks it was up and running. I was able to access John anytime, to make changes to the software that supported what I, an employee, needed to do. This is a stark contrast to the IT departments of most of the organizations I've encountered today. It was empowering for me, empowering for John, and resulted in technology being a supportive tool to being operationally effective.

Since those days over two decades ago at Magna, I've experienced, worked with, and even supported the integration of ERP and WMS systems that are a far cry from the customized versions I once worked with. The plethora of solutions in the marketplace today have made it easier to find solutions that are more closely aligned with the processes, steps, and outcomes of each operation, although sourcing functionality that supports efficiency for each individual operation is still a stretch.

There is also a conflict in the development of many software platforms today. If, for example, you were developing software to sell, it would make sense that the platform you built catered to as wide a variety of customers as possible. What this means to you and me is that the software is not structured to suit what we need, but is loosely constructed to be applicable to as many customers as possible. Tactically, this results in having to check boxes and do things that don't logically make sense when considering the outcome required. My advice here is to simply be wary of any software solution that is marketed as a solution built upon "best practices," mainly because the best practices for your organization are those found within your four walls.

My point is that *technology often influences an employee's ability to do the right things at the right time*, and not in a positive manner.

This isn't to say that all technology is bad, specifically ERP and WMS systems that are in the marketplace today. There are, as I described above, aspects of many systems today that can both support as well as hinder operational effectiveness. My experience, however, has been that for most of the solutions in the marketplace today, customizable solutions being the exception, there are more examples of the latter than the former, suggesting that if not selected and integrated correctly, technology can be more of a hindrance than a supportive tool.

As a fundamental building block of effective operations, there are considerations to make when identifying and integrating technology. Relative to both ERP and WMS solutions, I use a robust process with my clients to assist them in preparing for, identifying, sourcing, and integrating the best solution for their needs. What's also crucial about this approach is that I am not a salesperson for any software solution, nor do I purport to be one. It's been my experience that the selection and integration of the right solution is based on expertise in engaging the right people and optimizing business processes, more so than being an expert in software integration. Below I have outlined the nine phases of my approach at a high level. These nine steps will identify the best solution, ensure that the solution selected supports existing company best practices, and engage employees in the selection.

Here are the nine phases to achieving effective operations technology integration:

1. **Current state.** The existing work flow and business processes are documented and clearly understood. An understanding of the value stream is identified to incorporate the satisfaction of customer needs first and foremost.
2. **Validation.** All stakeholders, including end users (aka employees), confirm the accuracy and efficiency of existing processes. Any errors or omissions in the current state documentation are resolved.
3. **Optimization.** Ideas and recommendations for improvements to existing business processes and/or existing data collection and

reporting systems are clearly identified and captured. References to these ideas and recommendations are added to the current state documents.

4. **Sourcing.** A minimum of five separate ERP solutions are identified based on their ability to satisfy the criteria as outlined above. At this stage, sourcing is not based on budgetary constraints but built around satisfying the "optimum" solution as identified in phases one through three.

5. **Assessment.** ERP solutions are reviewed based on functionality, operation, and value, as it pertains to meeting the requirements captured in phases one through three. Employees and other various stakeholders are exposed to various demonstrations and on-site visits to organizations with the software already integrated and provide feedback and ideas for which solutions best suit the business needs.

6. **Decision.** The information gathered in phase five is used to narrow down the software solutions to meet the existing and perceived future business needs. Budget constraints are now considered based on the short list of solutions providers. When the solutions selected in phase four are not sufficient to satisfy the assessment phase and do not meet the budget criteria, additional solutions may be sourced.

7. **Planning.** A project plan is mapped out that incorporates the resources, knowledge, and time required to properly integrate the software. At this point additional resources and sound time-lines are outlined to ascertain exactly how long it will take and how much it will cost to fully integrate the software. Where the software can be split into phases (bite-sized chunks), planning will incorporate this.

8. **Testing and training.** During this phase stakeholders are introduced to the system in safe environments. Testing is not done in isolation of operations, but using real data and existing situations. Training is a mandatory component, and the project will not proceed until all users have experienced and provided input to the system.

9. **Introduction.** This is typically the last phase where the software is integrated into the operating environment. As outlined in phase eight, it is possible the system will be phased in, and where the solution is a significant undertaking, a pilot program may be initiated.

For more information on how to identify and integrate the optimum ERP or WMS system for your business, or for dozens of other resources to empower your operations, visit www.operational empowerment.com.

So what is the best technology?

To ensure that software acts as a supportive solution to optimize operational performance and effectiveness, it's crucial that its selection, testing, and introduction is done by the employees who use the system, not solely by those who work in IT. This may sound like a harsh statement, but I've repeatedly found that the most effective and powerful software introductions follow a similar approach to the nine phases I've identified above, and have very little involvement of IT until phase six, as IT must be able to ascertain if and how the solution will integrate with any other existing technologies.

3

Leading with Leverage

What the C-Suite Doesn't Know and How It Hurts Them

Early one wintery Saturday morning I was looking outside and finding it difficult to see the neighboring house that stood only a mere 50 feet away. The heavy snowfall and brisk and blowing winds had made it nearly impossible to see anything beyond the front door. I became mesmerized with the white flakes dancing in the sky, and tuned out of my surroundings as I considered the reality that we were homebound for yet another day. I quickly returned to reality when my four-year-old son said, "Daddy, look at that snow! There will be so much shoveling we can do today; when can we go outside?" My perceptions of the challenges that the rapidly falling snow presented were distinctly different from those of my son. We were looking at the same situation, but through very different lenses.

Peter F. Drucker once said, "So much of what we call management exists in making it difficult for people to work."[1] In my studies of both manufacturing and service-based organizations from around the globe, understanding and reaching consensus on the drivers behind poor operational performance can often seem difficult. I've found, for example, that if you incorporate interviews to uncover daily operational challenges, asking the same questions of frontline employees as you do managers, the responses you receive will often contain significantly different perspectives. In virtually every circumstance employees will identify the specific challenges they are facing and can demonstrate why they present such a challenge, whereas leaders within the same company will identify what they *believe* the challenges are that employees face in the daily operations, with little evidence to support their thesis. Of course, we discussed one of the key reasons why these perceptions can differ in my explanation of the operational disconnect in Chapter 1; however, it's important to drill down further to understand the significance of the operational disconnect as well as uncover several other drivers behind this gap in perceptions.

As a result of this likelihood of differences in opinion, to determine a true "current state" view of operational performance, and to avoid the influences of the operational disconnect, I often begin by asking the following questions of both management and employees:

1. What do your customers value in the company's products and/or services?
2. Which is more important to your customers: speed, quality, specifications, or response time?
3. What are the obstacles that diminish the company's ability to deliver value to customers?
4. What are the challenges that are reducing the ability to operate efficiently?
5. Where investment is required to improve operational effectiveness and efficiency?

Not surprisingly I've found that the more significant the gap is in responses one through three, the greater the risk of loss of business is, and the gap resulting from questions four and five correlates to the degree of employee disengagement and poor morale. Typically the differing opinions and viewpoints are not with intent. Senior management seeks to achieve the same objectives as the company's employees (serving customer needs and sustaining profitable growth), but there is a misunderstanding of what employees actually need to best serve the customers, resulting in senior management making misguided investments and decisions. We are looking at the same world through very different glasses.

Narrowing the Employee-Management Gap

There are three significant contributors that result in forging a disconnect between employees and management, the reduction of which will serve to form a stronger connection between those operating the business and those supporting the operations:

1. Lack of open dialogue between employees and management.
2. An inability to use *collaboration* effectively to increase productivity across the organization.
3. Failure to obtain and sustain organizational *accountability*.

A lack of open dialogue between employees and management is the most detrimental of all of these gaps, as its existence further exacerbates the severity of the remaining two gaps of collaboration and accountability. It is also the gap that can be most easily recognized simply by visiting and speaking with employees.

Building a Platform for Effective Dialogue

Historically, communications between senior management and employees have been in the form of e-mails, voice messages, and possibly even periodic presentations such as a town hall meeting. These approaches, although informative, are predominantly one-directional and do not facilitate discussion or serve to build a platform for effective dialogue. I recall participating as a manager in town hall sessions earlier in my career, escorting my employees to sit in on the town hall presented by the vice president. We knew in advance of the town hall discussions which employees were likely to speak up or become agitated and had discussed prior to the session how we might address any concerns.

In the event employees became disgruntled or conversations extended beyond cordial, the decision had been made that the vice president, or his directors, would return to presenting and ignore the individual as he or she was escorted from the room. The intent in these forums was to inform, not to discuss. Was this the best way to get the real issues out into the open?

The complexity of communicating effectively in today's multigenerational and multicultural workforce requires a more robust and multifaceted approach—a platform that facilitates collaborative dialogue across all levels of the organization. Failing to do so will only serve to increase the operational disconnect and reduce morale and productivity. How can you form this platform? In my work with clients from around the globe, we begin by engaging in the use of multichannel approaches to communication that facilitate broader discussions and an open dialogue consisting of the following four steps.

Communicate Across Multiple Channels

The options for communication today are much broader than only 10 short years ago, most of which are facilitated by technology. This doesn't take away from the value of face-to-face interactions, but it does provide additional methods to communicate information to ensure it is heard and understood. In addition, younger generations today are growing up accustomed to receiving electronic communications; hence their adoption of face or voice communications is very different from that of baby boomers or generation X.

> **Weekly news briefs.** Use e-mail as a means to communicate information summaries on the state of the business, new customer opportunities, to recognize employees, and to bring awareness to procedural changes or new hires. Every e-mail should end with an open invitation to hit "reply" to discuss concerns or ideas, and in turn any replies received should be treated as a priority and responded to.

Instant messaging. Let's be honest: picking up the phone, although a valuable communication means, can lead to longer conversations than are sometimes necessary. Texting and instant messaging, although reliant on the existence of technology to support their use, are a great means to facilitate rapid and brief information sharing across the organization. Once again the key is to solicit and respond to employee feedback and concerns as they arise.

Social media. Although you may want to dismiss social media as a communication channel, you should think again. Solutions such as those produced by Moxie[2] are changing how teams communicate by providing a platform for information sharing that improves upon e-mail and instant messaging.

Shift from Being Informative to Forming a Dialogue

It's rare that senior executives communicate with employees on a frequent basis; after all, everyone has a job to do. Herb Kelleher was known for frequent dialogues with employees during his tenure as CEO of Southwest Airlines. He would often show up unannounced in aircraft maintenance facilities, helping workers with their tasks. He would also help airline attendants on Southwest flights, distributing refreshments and talking with customers.[3] These frequent interactions placed Herb in the position of understanding the challenges and opportunities that employees faced, as well as facilitating dialogue with employees. Dialogues can occur organically through integration of the following activities:

Get in the trenches. Similar to Herb Kelleher's approach, invest time in meeting with and interacting with employees not only to understand what they do, but to mine their ideas on how it can be done better.

Get to know the person. Meeting with employees outside their work environment is just as important as meeting with them while they are at work. Personalized interactions provide insights into the challenges and opportunities faced outside of work that can yield new surprises. One of my clients was delighted to recently learn of a qualified engineer being on her staff. This information would never have come to light had she not made it a point of having a one-on-one discussion to learn more about the individual.

Make yourself available. A relationship of trust is built through personalized interactions and open dialogue. To facilitate this, it's critical that employee needs come first. We've all had a boss who let us know he or she was too busy to see us. I recall during a recent leadership forum a business owner advised that in order to increase productivity you should close your door more often. This is the wrong approach—employees are the horsepower of the business, therefore you have to make yourself available to discuss their concerns and ideas.

Create Predictable Frequency

Despite the value in incorporating these approaches to reduce the gap between senior executives and employees, finding the time to invest may seem like a challenge. Herein lies the third critical component of increasing the frequency and value of employee dialogues: creating a predictable frequency.

We are all wired for predictability, from what time we can expect to finish work to how long our next meeting will take. The degree of and desire for predictability varies by individual, but nonetheless it still exists. Albert-László Barabási, professor of physics at Northeastern University, and his team of scientists have been studying the predictability of humans for nearly a decade, reviewing different habits in travel. They have found that spontaneous individuals are largely absent from the population.[4] Making routine visits with employees on the frontlines, having scheduled "open door" hours, and holding meetings at regular intervals all form a predictable schedule that employees rely upon. Another practice that Tony Solecki, president of Caframo Limited, applies is to ensure that he and his senior staff hold one-on-one meetings with their employees every single week, with no excuses. "This is a key to our culture: ensuring employees have a private forum for their concerns, but doing so in a way that is predictable, so that all employees know they will have an opportunity to speak their mind."

Introducing Collaboration That's Productive

Next to a lack of open dialogue, insufficient or ineffective collaboration between management and employees is the second most significant influence that results in an employee-management gap. Insufficient collaboration can be easily recognized by any of the following issues that exist within the organization:

- New initiatives launched by senior management that fail to include consultation with employees.
- An unwillingness on behalf of senior management to rapidly resolve employee challenges.
- Low interest on the behalf of employees in supporting senior management initiatives.
- A lack of empowerment of employees to take action and resolve customer concerns.

For an extensive list of contributors to, and identification of, insufficient organizational collaboration, as well as dozens of other resources to empower your operation, visit www.operationalempowerment.com.

Collaboration may seem to be an overused metaphor with little substance, but when considered relative to business operations, collaboration becomes an integral and necessary component of ensuring all levels and individuals across the organization work together to achieve the common objective of providing meaningful value to the customer. This is the essence of productive collaboration.

There are several stages to achieving productive collaboration (Figure 3.1), working in conjunction with one another in support of rapidly disseminating and converging on a singular vision and direction.

FIGURE 3.1 Productive Collaboration

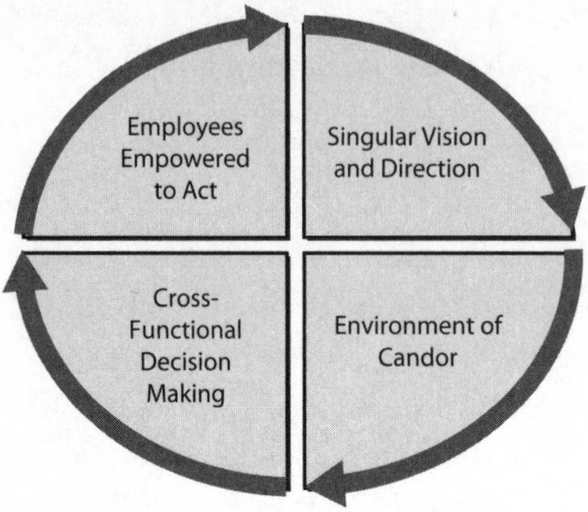

Phase 1: Form a Singular Direction

There is a naturally occurring conflict that can arise amid senior management teams, which if unnoticed or ill managed can serve to extinguish collaboration before it ever begins. This conflict exists when executives are driven to achieve goals and objectives, and in some instances compensated to deliver on specific goals and objectives that are not in direct alignment with the goals and objectives of others. If the vice president of sales, for example, is responsible for closing sales without consideration of the costs of doing so, and the CFO's mandate is to control or reduce costs, then a conflict will inevitably arise between these individuals. Objectives that are independent of one another create conflicts that diminish collaboration. Worse yet, conflicts that exist at the executive level most often trickle down to poison the employees who work in the same departments.

Achieving a singular direction requires that executive and departmental objectives be created in unison. Here is an example:

Conflicting Individual Corporate Objectives

Vice President of Sales: Achieve 5 percent revenue growth across North America in the next 24 months.

CFO: Reduce costs of managing North American operation by 10 percent in the next 24 months.

Collaborative Corporate Objectives

> *Vice President of Sales: Increase sales by 5 percent across North America while supporting reduced costs in the same region in the next 24 months.*

> *CFO: Identify 10 percent cost reduction opportunities across North America that have no impact on sales growth in the next 24 months.*

By formulating collaborative objectives and targets, we create a singular direction for the organization that starts at the executive level and slowly trickles down throughout the company. There are fewer opportunities for conflict to arise when objectives coincide and support one another.

Phase 2: Create an Environment of Candor

Willingness to openly share and contribute ideas cannot exist unless there is inherent candor across all levels of leadership within an organization. For many of the business owners and executives that I advise, we spend time discussing how to introduce candor as a means to open up communication channels, building trust and an environment where collaboration can exist. In *Creativity, Inc.*,[5] author Ed Catmull outlines how Pixar formed the Braintrust as a means of creating an environment for reviewing and improving upon movie projects through problem solving and collaboration. The results of this type of open and candid environment can be experienced through viewing any of Pixar's films.

Building a culture of candor requires leaders who are willing to speak openly about their views, but more important listen to the views and opinions of their employees. This makes employees comfortable with sharing their views and ideas. Through nurturing an environment of candor, collaboration can yield powerful results, as those involved have become accustomed to sharing without holding back, and believing in the value of their views and opinions.

Phase 3: Initiate Cross-Functional Decision Making

Decisions that are made in silos stay in silos. The most effective decisions are those that transcend across the organization involving input and contribution from various functional groups. Through integration of various stakeholders, those both directly and indirectly involved in the decision-making process, we create decisions that serve to achieve the following:

- Consider all aspects and perspectives relative to the situation at hand
- Provide new insights and ideas that may not have been considered otherwise
- Form the basis for commitment to the agreed-upon outcome

It's this final point that yields the greatest value. Whether a decision aligns with an individual's needs or meets with his or her desires is irrelevant. By simply being a part of the decision-making process, individuals have a greater understanding of the issues at hand, gain a broader perspective relative to influencing factors and other important considerations, and perceive the outcome as something they've been a part of. This is the very basis by which our electoral candidates are brought into office. By being inclusive of the general public, allowing voters the opportunity to speak their mind, elected officials have a greater chance at being accepted than if they were simply selected by the former administration and placed into office.

Phase 4: Empower Employees to Take Action

Collaboration cannot be productive without enabling the employees to take action. I spent some time working with a large international beverage company because its new managers felt overwhelmed. As pressures mounted from the executive team to improve productivity and reduce downtime in their plants, managers on the front lines were feeling pressure to increase production while reducing quality problems and defects. The result was that the new managers took on more and more responsibility themselves rather than engaging with and empowering employees. Once I was engaged and began interviewing the frontline managers, it became clear that their reasoning for lack of engaging with employees was a concern that if responsibilities were handed over to employees there would be lack of control and a greater chance for errors and problems.

Empowerment must exist at all levels of the organization for productive collaboration to be effective. This means that the operational environment must be one that includes the following:

- Employees are encouraged to make decisions on their own, without engaging management.
- Decisions that seem to contradict current work practices are made inclusive of others.
- Mistakes that are made while introducing changes and improvements are not punished, but accepted and learned from.
- A significant amount of effort is invested in training, knowledge and skill building, and cross-functional development.

By introducing the four phases above, productive collaboration becomes a self-sustaining approach to making more robust operational decisions; ensuring buy-in and commitment across all levels of the organization; and creating a sense of urgency and empowerment to take rapid action on the identified actions to yield the desired results.

Sustaining Accountability

Early in my career I worked for a very respectable and highly intelligent COO who was a master at holding others accountable. He had a memory like an elephant, never forgetting the commitments others made to him, and more important never letting anyone off the hook for a failure to follow through on his or her commitment. Although these are the foundational aspects of forming a community of accountability, there was one weakness that was detrimental to his approach. When anyone failed to meet a commitment, the COO became highly agitated to the point that virtually everyone around him was uncomfortable. This growing discomfort turned into resentment and quickly diminished any respect employees held for the COO. His tenure within the company was short once resentment reached a breaking point for the CEO and the employees.

Accountability cannot, and will not, exist without first ensuring that sufficient organizational communication exists, in conjunction with productive collaboration. More specifically, it's virtually impossible to hold someone accountable if we haven't first set clear expectations that the person understands and agrees to, and then provided the necessary support to ensure that the person can achieve these expectations. Accountability is not about setting employees up for failure, but supporting them in their success, and there are few employees that will not agree to being held accountable if they truly believe you have their best interests in mind.

In order to build and sustain an operational environment of accountability you must ensure that there is:

1. Clear communication surrounding organizational role objectives, expectations, and responsibilities
2. Alignment across role objectives in support of departmental and organizational objectives
3. The tools, resources, and environment that support achieving the objectives and expectations
4. The desire and support across the business to work collaboratively toward achieving objectives
5. Clear methods to measure and monitor progression toward objectives
6. Prompt feedback and discussions relative to progress or lack thereof

Barbara Zeins, president of Gerson and Gerson, had invested a significant amount of time in improving communication across the company and introducing a collaborative team environment. She shifted employees from working in silos and areas of specialty into smaller teams in order to best serve their customer and to ensure more collaborative goals and targets were formed. Although this shift brought significant value to customers and the company, our work together to design organizational role objectives working in conjunction with employees and managers was the final element to ensure more productive collaboration. It was through this process that we were able to create both qualitative and quantitative measures of individual and team performance, and it wasn't until these role objectives were clearly documented and introduced that accountability became measureable. And as we all know, what is measured gets done.

Nurturing Your Most Valued Players

Employees are the horsepower behind a business operation. Ergo, without employees it would be impossible to deliver on commitments to customers. In fact, it's unlikely you would even make commitments to customers. It's for this reason that I refer to any employee as a business's Most Valuable Player, or MVP for short. This statement has two aspects to consider.

First and foremost, employees are, for any business, the means by which value is identified, delivered, and served to customers:

- A failure to sustain a sufficient number of employees to service customer needs will lead to the demise of a business.
- Employing those who have a poor attitude or misguided belief as to how to best serve and support the customer will lead to the demise of the business.
- Having employees who are unskilled in delivering the products or services that the business seeks to provide to its customers will lead to the demise of the business.

As a frequent flyer, I travel on numerous airlines around the world. As a result I collect air miles with several of my preferred carriers. It was only recently that I decided to investigate cashing in such miles with Air Canada, which I use as my preferred carrier when I travel in Canada. After visiting the Aeroplan website, I was directed to call a toll-free number, and to my astonishment, once I navigated my way through the menu I received a message that said (and I'm sure you know what's coming),

"All of our attendants are busy, but will be happy to serve you shortly. The current wait time is one hour and 15 minutes." Just how long do you think customers of the Aeroplan program with Air Canada will tolerate hold times of more than one hour to have their questions answered? My guess: not long. Yet the only trigger that is likely to drive Air Canada to make any changes in the processes and resources it has in support of its customer call center, is when it begins to see lost revenue from those disengaging from its air miles program. Lost revenue is often the only clear metric that is watched closely by both executives and board members, and despite the likely feedback that employees and frontline leaders have provided about their inability to effectively manage the inbound call volume, nothing is likely to change until a key business metric such as revenue or possibly customer complaints hits senior management's radar. This is the employee-management gap at work.

The second question that should come to mind when considering employees as your Most Valuable Players is, do your employees *feel* valuable? More important, what makes an employee feel valued?

If we consider that value is in the eye of the beholder, then it's safe to presume that there are dozens if not hundreds of perceptions as to what value is. Herein lies the complexity of trying to ensure that employees feel valued: the options are simply too broad. I've seen even small businesses of only 15 to 20 employees struggle with trying to make employees feel valued. What is valuable to one employee may be distinctly different for another employee.

Unfortunately, in the broad array of choices that senior management has to make in trying to make employees feel valued, a choice often results in drawing upon a limited number of generalizations rather than an assessment of actual feedback. The most common assumptions made are that employees generally value money, time, job security, and predictability. These are valid assumptions if we are to lead by way of Maslow's hierarchy formed in the 1940s.[6] Unfortunately these types of generalizations don't address why employees are spending less time at their jobs than ever before. The U.S. Bureau of Labor Statistics reported in 2012 that employed persons between the ages of 18 and 46 would have 11.3 jobs during their career. Assuming that most people will work for 35 years, this means a new job every three years, and this number is diminishing as we see more millennials join the workforce. [7]

If we move away from generalizations and look to specifics, we find that recent studies, such as the Gallup study mentioned earlier, [8] have found that most employees leave for the same reasons:

- 31.5 percent cite a lack of advancement or promotional opportunity.
- 20.2 percent cite a lack of job fit.
- 16.5 percent leave due to management or the general work environment.

This research, along with countless other studies showing similar results, suggests that regardless of how much money and communication senior management provides to employees that supports long-term job security, it will fail to have any significant impact on employee retention. It also becomes apparent that the reason employees leave is that they feel a disconnection with the business, be it in their role, with their boss, or based on their skill level. To narrow this gap and create a stronger connection between employees and the business, senior management must integrate methods to empower employees to maximize operational performance and effectiveness. Consider, for example, how empowerment would support this objective when contrasted against each of the three reasons mentioned above as to why employees leave.

Empowerment Exposes Employees to New Skills

Empowering employees exposes them to new skills that would alleviate some of the desire for advancement and promotional opportunities. In an operational role where tasks and responsibilities are often repetitive, it can be quite common for employees to feel stagnant as a result of the limited scope of their position and therefore the restriction in career options. If introduced correctly, empowerment will expose employees to new skill sets, new ideas, and a broad array of knowledge that furthers an understanding of the business and the opportunities that exist within it.

Group Decision Making Broadens Perspectives

Empowering employees to make cross-functional decisions will allow them a better understanding of the various roles and responsibilities of their coworkers. A lack of job fit is often a perception based on having limited exposure to other areas of the business. As a result, a belief is generated in the employee that "the grass is greener" on the outside of the business. Through my coaching of many business leaders and middle managers I've found that specific to an operational role, where the pace of work and demands and expectations can be high, employees often determine that their specific role is limited in scope, and therefore form a desire to seek other opportunities outside of the organization. Where employees are empowered to work together in cross-functional teams, the lines of demarcation between various roles becomes blurred as employees learn to work as a team or unit rather than as individual contributors.

Empowerment Demands a Change in Leadership Style

Forming an environment of empowerment requires a different management style, and hence has a direct impact on the work environment. In an empowered work environment, frontline leaders and middle management must shift from managing tasks and people to focusing on the continued development of their people and the effectiveness of their team as a unit. As leaders shift from telling employees "what they should be doing" toward "supporting employees in achieving what must be done," the barriers between leadership and employees are broken down.

The Toro Company is a great example of an organization that recognizes its most valuable players. Having been around since 1914, Toro has gone through a number of evolutions as the market and its competition have shifted. Despite this, it still has a high number of employees who have been with the company 10, 20, and even 30 years. The Toro Company has built its business on something it calls the Pride in Excellence model.[9] I've already discussed my personal bias against using the word *excellence* in Chapter 1; however, setting this aside, the essence of the model supports putting Toro's MVPs first, combining people values with performance values to achieve the Toro vision. People come first, and in order to support the company's people values, senior leadership at Toro promotes the idea of teamwork, empowerment, and communication. In doing so Toro has been able to ensure not only that long-tenured employees remain at Toro, but also quality and consistency in how its products are manufactured and brought to market, the continued satisfaction of its customers, and an ability to sustain its market position.

PART 2

Focus and Momentum Equate to Operational Power

Now that we have discussed the foundational components to an effective and profitable operation, it goes without saying that we have to create a plan and momentum around it in order to propel the operation forward.

In Part 2, I will present a proven method to develop a vision and strategic plan that will ensure commitment and action, supporting the capitalization on your investment in a strong foundation. More specifically, I will discuss how to engage your employees, customers, and other key stakeholders to support your plan, allowing you to rapidly increase the velocity by which you achieve the strategy.

Part 2 is more than just setting a plan, it's laying the groundwork to dramatically and rapidly increase the effectiveness of your operation.

4

Strategic Strings

Helping Employees Connect with Your Vision

Setting a vision for the future of an organization is not and should not be an isolated event or considered top secret. Your vision of the future, regardless of the destination, is something that must have meaning and be relevant and significant to your employees. After all, they are ultimately responsible for delivering value to your customers that in turn will help you achieve this vision.

In this chapter we will discuss the *operational opportunity* that is derived from ensuring that employees understand and connect with the desired direction of the company, and outline exactly how to make this connection using my six-step approach.

If you feel comfortable that you already have a solid foundation upon which to improve operational performance (if not, see Chapter 2), then this chapter will help you identify and take the specific steps necessary to capitalize on your investment in time and resources in order to formulate and achieve your vision.

Before you proceed, however, I urge you to ensure that you're comfortable with Chapters 2 and 3, which will provide you with a sufficient foundation for moving into Chapter 4. Attempting to integrate the ideas and methodologies I suggest in this chapter without having a proper foundation would be like trying to float a boat with a hole in the hull.

Use Your Vision Statement to Define Your Future

If you read the vision statements of most companies today you will find a vast array, many of which aren't worth the paper they are written on. Sound harsh? It should. A vision statement is a decision-making tool that must have meaning to both customers (prospective and existing) and employees. It's the former group that the vision is meant to serve, and it's the latter group that will deliver on the vision. Deciphering between vision statements that are actually marketing fluff and those that have true meaning to the audience they are intended to speak to, requires the application of what I call the "So what?" test. It's likely easier if I demonstrate this test rather than explain it.

Consider Dell's vision statement (as of this writing): "*To be the most successful computer company in the world at delivering the best customer experience in markets we serve.*" What exactly does this vision statement mean? What does success look like? What exactly does the "best customer service" look like? What markets are we serving, and what are the distinct differences in each market? This vision statement begs the question, "So what?" Frankly this statement wouldn't inspire any employee because it is too vague and based on a series of generalities. It is marketing-focused rather than people-focused.

Now let's look at McDonald's vision statement: "*McDonald's vision is to be the world's best quick service restaurant experience. Being the best means providing outstanding quality, service, cleanliness, and value, so that we make every customer in every restaurant smile.*" Is this vision statement specific and measurable? More important, can employees understand from this vision statement exactly what it is that they need to achieve in order to deliver consistent value to their customer? Absolutely.

In the simplest of terms, a vision statement is meant to describe the ideal future state of the organization. It is the chosen destination, and to serve as such it must meet the following criteria:

> **Expressive.** A vision statement must effectively convey the desired future position of an organization that extends well beyond the

boardroom. The vision must be something that is meaningful to those parties external to the company, such as customers and supplier partners, as well as those internal to the company, including executives, managers, and most important, employees. This latter group is most crucial to the success of the vision if it is going to be achieved, therefore the vision must convey the meaning not only of where the organization intends to be, but specifically what it will look like in order to achieve this vision.

Definitive. Motivational speakers such as Tony Robbins, Jack Canfield, and Zig Ziglar have been touting the benefits of goal setting for decades. The key to achieving a goal is ensuring it is definitive in describing the desired future state. Refer back to McDonald's vision statement, and notice the last statement: *"so that we make every customer in every restaurant smile."* Not only is this statement definitive, but it reaches a level that each and every executive, store owner, manager, and employee can relate to.

Measurable. How is it possible to determine whether you achieve your vision? After all, is a vision meant to be an elusive goal? Hardly. Believe it or not, the most powerful visions are those that can be achieved, and measurably so. In order to ensure that the vision provides meaning to those who are responsible for its attainment, it must include measures of success. Consider Amazon's vision statement: *"Our [Amazon's] vision is to be earth's most customer centric company; to build a place where people can come to find and discover anything they might want to buy online."* This is another great example of a powerful vision statement that is not only expressive and definitive but measurable. Once Amazon has identified and integrated the ability to sell all products that its customers may want to buy online, its vision has been achieved. It will be at this point that the company should revisit its vision. Any customer, supplier, executive, or employee can clearly understand what it is that Amazon is trying to achieve, and they can measure for themselves when that vision is achieved.

You may have noticed a pattern through each of these criteria. A vision statement must have meaning not only to customers and executives but to *employees*. Before you can ever engage and empower your employees, they must feel aligned with the vision of the company and have a means of effectively measuring their contribution toward the vision. To achieve this requires input and validation from employees as to whether the vision statement portrays meaning, and this must happen *before* the vision statement is designed and finalized. Formulating a vision statement is not something to be done in secrecy, but an activity that must engage employees in envisioning the future of the company.

Based on my work with clients in forming their vision statement, here are the five steps to obtain and incorporate employee ideas and input into the formulation of a vision statement:

1. **Solicit ideas.** Where should the company be heading, and what are the opportunities?
2. **Involve employees.** Get their input into the formulation of the vision.
3. **Communicate options.** Present several options to employees for their feedback.
4. **Validate the results.** Take the draft to employees for their input on whether the vision is expressive, definitive, and measurable.
5. **Communicate contribution.** Each team or work group should clearly understand how group members contribute to the vision and their roles and responsibilities.

Engagement Before Objectives: Why Employees Must Be Involved in Strategy Formulation

Several years ago I was assisting Larsen and Shaw, a family-owned business, in formulating its strategy, a process the company had engaged in every three years for over a decade. The company had always brought in an outside facilitator and had generally been pleased with the results. During our initial meetings to discuss the formulation session, I asked John Larsen (then president) and Mary Jane Bushell (then vice president of operations) which frontline leaders they would like me to speak to. My question was intriguing to the president because as long as he had owned the business he had not involved frontline leadership early on in strategy formulation. This was not on purpose or by design; it had simply never been a request from previous facilitators.

With the names of several key employees in hand, I reached out and interviewed more than a half-dozen to obtain their thoughts and ideas on what was working well in the business and what were some of the existing challenges in meeting company and customer objectives. Following the discussions I sorted the information into categories identifying both similarities and differences in opinions. This information provided the groundwork for me to begin the strategy formulation session with the senior leadership team.

After reading the comments and concerns, John turned to me and said, "Shawn, this is the first time we have ever asked frontline leaders for their ideas *before* we commenced our strategic planning session, and to be frank I'm not sure why we waited until now."

Obtaining employee input to a strategy is critical. Why? Primarily because employees are those most closely connected with the business operations and the customer. Think of it like this. If equipment, a business process, or even a piece of software is not functioning as efficiently or effectively as it could, creating bottlenecks or delays in delivering products or services, would senior management know? It's possible, but as I discussed earlier, most of the information and feedback from employees on the front lines is filtered as it is communicated upward, resulting in the operational disconnect. If employees complain that a piece of equipment runs slowly, their team leaders, supervisors, or managers may or may not act on improving the equipment speed depending on:

1. Their understanding of how the equipment is intended to function (i.e., does the equipment operate at this speed for a reason?).
2. Their current priorities (i.e., do they have other, more pressing priorities that need to be addressed?).
3. Their relationship with the employee (i.e., is this an employee whose opinion the supervisor or manager respects?).

4. The feedback they receive from peers (i.e., did maintenance confirm that the operating speed is at the optimum rate?).

5. Their belief that senior management will respond (i.e., will their requests for improved speed or efficiency from the equipment fall on deaf ears?).

Because of these biases, it's crucial that ideas and concerns come directly from employees without filter, in a nonthreatening, confidential environment.

Peter Drucker once said, "Employees will only complain or make suggestions three times on the average without a response. After that they conclude that if they don't keep quiet they will be thought to be troublemakers or that management doesn't care." This brings about the second reason as to why employee input is crucial to the success of any strategy. The more frequently we can engage and dialogue with employees regarding our business strategy, the less it becomes a "senior management initiative" and the greater the chances that it will be perceived as a means to "help *us* achieve our desired future." Engage employees early in the strategy formulation process, and they will be more engaged and committed to the objectives and actions. In essence, early involvement helps employees connect the strategy with their individual goals and objectives, which in turn feeds the strategy.

The last—and I would suggest most crucial—reason to involve employees early in the strategy formulation session is for diversity of input. The most valuable and sound strategies are built upon diversity of opinion creating a broad view of the business, the customer, and the market. A strategy that is formulated by a board or senior executives does have value, but it lacks robustness. The board's view is often the result of information provided by senior executives, and the senior executives' views are often the result of unqualified information that has been provided by managers and supervisors. In addition, members of a board or senior management team often spend a considerable amount of time interacting with one another, both inside and outside of work. This is obviously necessary in order to build a strong bond; however, there's a fine line between building a bond among executives and minimizing the diversity and creativity of the team. Groups that spend considerable time together generally fall prey to groupthink, which can lead to one-sided views that have little value or consideration of the environment. I've also found through my personal experience that many CEOs or presidents have a strong view on where their company should be focused, and hence they dominate the strategy session with their views. The more dominant the CEO or president, the less chance there is that the strategy will be sufficient to support future growth and improvement.

Early involvement of employees creates the engagement necessary to form a distinct competitive advantage that results from a robust strategy built upon diverse, customer-focused, real-time, and relevant ideas.

More Than Ideas: From SWOT to SWEAT

The SWOT analysis (assessing a business's strengths, weaknesses, opportunities, and threats) has long been a staple of the strategic formulation process, often being credited to the work of Albert S. Humphrey.[1] Despite its validity as a tool to be used in understanding and analyzing the current state of a business, its application provides little insight into exactly what we should do with the information that's been identified. Should a strength, for example, be capitalized on or merely set aside in favor of pursuing an opportunity? Should we invest any energy at all into lessening the impact of a weakness, or be more conscious of minimizing threats? The answers to these questions will vary depending on who is leading the strategy—for example, I'm a proponent of capitalizing on strengths (they are what got us to where we are in the first place) and aggressively pursuing opportunities (they are our best means to accomplishing our vision), while downplaying irrelevant weaknesses in favor of placing remaining efforts into managing urgent threats. I've found repeatedly that this is the best approach to rapidly pursuing organizational goals, while minimizing distractions and wasted effort.

Of course, this isn't the only school of thinking when it comes to applying a SWOT analysis.

What I suggest that you do with the information is less important than how you obtain the information. Applied correctly, a SWOT analysis (and other tools such as a Horizon Scan) enables a collective view of the organization's current and future positioning in the marketplace. As I alluded to earlier, it's through the diversity of opinion that we gain a holistic understanding of the state of the business, its customers, and the market; with a diversity of opinion comes disagreement and misinterpretation. To maximize the value of diversity, a collaborative approach must be enacted to create a singular vision of the current and future state of the business.

If you've ever seen the classic movie *Twelve Angry Men*,[2] then you've witnessed firsthand both the power and the value in diversity of opinion. In the movie, Henry Fonda is the sole juror with the belief that a young man is innocent of murdering his father. As the movie progresses, Fonda is joined by other jurors who begin to see the evidence in a new light, impacting their opinions as to the guilt of the accused. Despite the varying backgrounds, personalities, and opinions of the jurors, through collaboration they are able to reach a better decision. It's not the evidence, the circumstances, or even Fonda that make a difference in swaying the jurors' decisions; it's the power of collaboration.

In formulating a strategy, collaboration yields the most valuable outcomes. The greater the diversity of the group however, the more difficult achieving collaboration becomes, which in turn is why most companies today fail to attempt to broaden the diversity of their strategy formulation beyond the boardroom. However, not only is the effort valuable in yielding more significant outcomes, but also through collaboration we create the early engagement and alignment necessary to support rapid and committed action to deliver on the strategy.

So although a SWOT analysis (and other similar tools) can yield valuable ideas about the business in its current or future state, how the tool is applied is considerably more important than the specific information it provides. This brings me to my next point: the majority of companies fail to achieve their strategies.[3] So despite the best of efforts in collecting and assessing information relative to the business's current and future state, we are still failing to address the most significant challenge of all, which is acting on the strategy. As I mentioned earlier, a collaborative approach to formulating strategy is a precursor to delivering on the vision, but we need to have a more definitive means to *achieve our strategy*. It's for this reason that I use the SWEAT method to formulate strategy.

By incorporating the power of a SWOT analysis with the components to build collaboration and a mechanism to ensure clear and powerful actions, we can ensure that every strategy is a successful one. I've captured these ideas in an acronym I've aptly named SWEAT, which stands for strengths, weaknesses, employee input, action plans, and thrust. My guess is that the first thing you'll notice is the explicit absence of "opportunities" and "threats" in this model as compared to a SWOT analysis, and for good reason. If you've ever performed a SWOT analysis of any kind, you've probably found there is a blurred line between strengths versus opportunities and weaknesses versus threats. What I consider a strength, for example, you may invariably consider an opportunity, and who am I to argue (and why waste energy doing so)? In the SWEAT approach to strategy formulation, the power is in slowly building collaboration around the current state, future state, *and* action plans necessary to move the business forward and achieve the vision.

Here is a more definitive description of the SWEAT approach to strategy formulation.

Strengths
Collectively identify the strengths of the business, both in its present state and in its desired future state. These strengths include considerations of resources, capital, equipment, technology, customer relationships, product or service distinction, market positioning, global reach, and employee talent. Strengths are best captured during interviews with key stakeholders prior to the strategy session, as well as by collectively reviewing, discussing, and documenting during the session.

Here are my preferences for key sources of identifying business strengths:

- **Customers.** Identify what customers enjoy about the company's products or services; specifically, why do they keep coming back?
- **Suppliers and contractors.** What do key suppliers perceive as the strength of the company? When compared to other similar companies, what do suppliers see as the key strategic or competitive advantages or strengths of the business?
- **Partnerships and alliances.** Why have other companies or professionals chosen to partner with the business today? What value does the business bring to their practice, company, customers, or employees? Where do the greatest opportunities exist for the partnership to further exploit existing or untapped opportunities?
- **Board members and volunteers.** Why do these individuals continuously support the company through their volunteer efforts? What do they perceive are the greatest strengths of the business today, and what further opportunities exist tomorrow?
- **Spouses and significant others of employees.** What benefit does the company provide your family and your community? What are the strengths of the company today that keep your spouse or significant other coming back to work day after day? What drives your spouse to want to work with the company in the future?
- **Employees.** See "Employee Input" below.

Weaknesses

Recognize and document the imperfections, fragilities, and shortcomings of the business, both in its current state and in the future if the direction remains consistent. Weaknesses encompass threats to the business (those things that are being undermanaged or not considered in day-to-day operations), as well as competitors, products, or service fragilities, shifts in customer preferences, gaps in talent, employee distrust, concerns with product or service quality, and lack of resources.

Identifying weaknesses is by far the easiest task for any business executive, owner, or employee. After all, we are creatures of correction—always seeking out problems in an effort to bring solutions. It's for this reason that I find weaknesses tend to fall out in "strength" interviews naturally, and as they are often twice as numerous as strengths, only need to be discussed before the strategy session with participants and employees, and during the strategy formulation session itself.

Employee Input

Input and ideas should be obtained from employees at various points throughout the strategy formulation. Of course, employees offer significant ideas and inputs to identify the strengths and weaknesses of the business, but they should also be engaged during the formulation of objectives and action plans, and on an ongoing basis as the strategy is rolled out.

The approach to obtaining employee input can vary by company. For example:

> **Small to midsize enterprise.** A combination of formal and informal interviews conducted both on-site and off-site offer insights into the current state of the business. It's crucial that a combination of approaches be used in these environments, as both a closer bond and concern over lack of confidentiality will exist in a smaller group.
> **Large enterprise.** Formal interviews across a variety of departments and divisions are best used to identify trends, commonalities, and distinct opportunities and threats. In this approach employees should be given advance notice of the interviews, allowing them time to prepare. The distance from the central organization creates a greater feeling of confidentiality and hence diminishes the necessity for informal interviews. It's also necessary in an organization of this magnitude to ensure consistency in approach so as not to inadvertently harm relationships or undermine trust.
> **Global organization.** Similar to large enterprises, the key in global organizations is ensuring formality and consistency. It is

necessary, however, to also consider cultural norms; for example, the approach to arranging and conducting a "formal" interview in a New York–based business might be seen as less desirable when applied to a business located in Asia or India.

Although questions can vary depending on needs, the key considerations in order to ensure sufficient information to support strategy formulation include operational performance gaps as they relate to employees, equipment, or technology weaknesses; inconsistencies in how executives and management deal with employees, equipment, or technology weaknesses; customer and market opportunities; product manufacturing or service delivery weaknesses; and labor discontent or unrest. Similar to the approaches mentioned above, diversity of employee input is key to ensuring that a clear picture of the current state of the business is understood.

Action Plans

According to Dr. Kotter,[4] about 5 percent of all strategies are successfully implemented, nearly 70 percent of all strategic initiatives fail, and the remaining 25 percent have some success but never fully achieve the potential of the strategy devised.[5] These are pretty dismal statistics, but not that unusual when you consider how strategic action plans are formed, rolled out, and monitored as we've discussed above.

The most successful action plans are built upon three fundamental elements, namely:

- What is to be done?
- Who will be responsible for doing it?
- When will it be done by?

This is the "What, by Whom, by When" approach to action planning. Specifically, for every significant action that is to be taken, it has to be clear what is being done, who is responsible for doing it, and when it will be complete. To ensure that our strategy is successful, it's crucial that we apply a similar methodology to achieve our strategic objectives and to drive accountability across the organization, as accountability breeds commitment *and* engagement in employees at all levels. Here is my four-step approach to building action plans that breed accountability and achieve results:

1. **Clarity of actions.** Are the actions clearly stated, minimizing errors in interpretation and allowing for clear measurement of completion?

   Example of unclear action:
   Have all procedures revised and updated by December 31.

   Example of a clear action:
   Review, revise (if necessary,) and reissue all Boring Mill procedures to Production teams by December 31.

2. **Congruence of actions.** Do the actions align with the direction of the organization as it pertains to the vision and strategic objectives? Do they make sense to those responsible for completing them?

   Example of an incongruent action:
   Action 1: Review inventory replenishment procedures and confirm cycle counting details are included.
   Action 2: Update all inventory procedures to replace cycle counting with physical counts where necessary.

   Example of a congruent action:
   Action 1: Review inventory replenishment procedures to confirm details on inventory counts are included.
   Action 2: Update or revise procedures to ensure the appropriate counting method is included (i.e., cycle counting for small high-turn components; physical counts for larger slow-moving inventory).

3. **Empowerment to take action.** Are those involved in executing action plans empowered to act upon the actions they are executing, or does a lack of seniority, lack of knowledge, or conflicting levels of authority disempower their mobility?

Example of a disempowered action:
Review overdue membership accounts, bringing those accounts over 30 days to the attention of the Manager, Membership.

Example of an empowered action:
Review and contact directly all membership accounts greater than 30 days past due. Use calling script procedure 123 and document all responses for follow-up with the Manager, Membership.

Building powerful action plans that incorporate a "What, by Whom, by When" approach built around clarity, congruence, and empowerment ensures that actions are completed thoroughly and on time.

Strategic Thrust

To reach orbit, every rocket must propel itself through the atmosphere at a blistering pace. As the journey progresses and the destination becomes closer, the degree of thrust is lessened, replaced by smaller and less significant propulsion adjustments. This is the same theory that must be applied to a business strategy if it is going to be achieved. With a collaborative strategy formulated and clear action plans in place using the aforementioned approach, it's necessary to create significant thrust in the direction of the objectives to move the strategy forward. In order to do so, it's critical to first assess past performance, expectations, and barriers in order to ensure that less-than-adequate performance is addressed before the strategy is initiated (Figure 4.1). The areas that should be considered include the following five points:

Employee expectations. What have employees come to expect relative to how successful the organization is at introducing and achieving change initiatives? Any biases will have to be overcome.
Demands of organized labor. What are the expectations, demands, or policies of organized labor (if in existence) that must be taken into account? Plans should be presented or reviewed in

a manner that facilitates engagement rather than creating barriers in relationships or communication.

Historic business performance. How well have we done historically at delivering on our strategy? If we've failed in previous attempts, what needs to change in order to achieve success? What external and internal influences may have impacted our ability to deliver?

Social and cultural norms. Are there specific means by which the strategy should be communicated or introduced across various cultures or divisions to ensure that a clear and consistent message is received by all? Have we considered all of the social and cultural norms during the formulation of the strategy? If so, how should we best communicate this?

Market and competitive expectations. What do our customers, competitors, and investors expect from us? What biases might exist that we need to address or overcome?

FIGURE 4.1 Barriers to a Successful Strategy Implementation

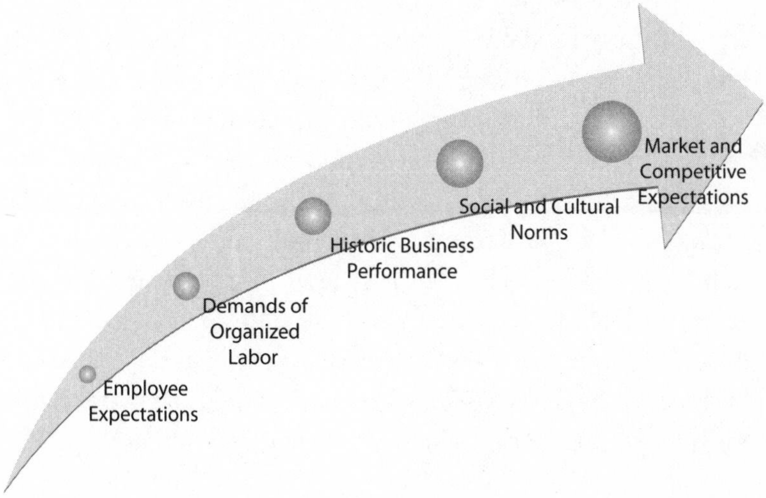

To achieve a vision requires consideration of past performance as identified through reflecting on the five points mentioned above. With this reflection, complete strategic thrust can then be created from assessing and incorporating the following four key areas:

1. **Identify low-hanging fruit.** For every strategic objective, what is the most powerful action that will yield the most visual results? This should be an action that can easily be achieved but represents a significant shift in how the business is operating.

2. **Engage key stakeholders.** Who are the natural cheerleaders in the company today? Selecting those people who are enthusiastic about change *and* respected by others, and engaging them in the initial actions, will ensure not only successful outcomes but also indirect marketing across the business as to the powerful future they are part of, thereby creating interest and intrigue in other employees.

3. **Promote and share success.** As the old saying goes, if you don't toot your own horn there is no music. Achieving success, regardless of how small, as you progress through strategic action plans is something to celebrate and advertise. This promotion of success helps to engage employees not only in what you are trying to achieve but also in the ability to follow through and achieve results.

4. **Recruit.** In 2011, the U.S. military spent an estimated $667 million dollars on advertising.[6] This may seem astronomical, but when you consider that the military would not exist if not for its ability to recruit top talent, the investment suddenly seems rudimentary to the outcomes it produces. It's logically quite difficult to recruit on the heels of a failed mission, but if you consider the successes the U.S. military has had, as well as the lifestyle and opportunities a military career can offer, its position and timing couldn't be more impeccable. This is the same theory that you must apply to engaging employees in strategic action plans. With successes promoted and shared across the business, the time is right to recruit more volunteers.

Through a focus on these four areas you can build and sustain strategic thrust to ensure that your strategy gets off the ground and has the speed and velocity necessary to survive over the long term, and the ability to achieve the desired outcomes.

Measurement in Strategy Alone Doesn't Equate to Outcomes

Peter Drucker once said, "What gets measured gets managed." If Peter were with us today, I think he might change his tune. With the advent of "big data," executives and managers have been bombarded with all sorts of data, but amidst the cacophony of information we are left pondering several questions:

> **Is the information correct?** Garbage in equates to garbage out, and before we make assumptions and take action based on what data is telling us, we want to be sure that the inputs are correct.
>
> **Which information is of greatest value?** With options to slice and dice information in so many ways, one has to ask: What information provides the details that we need?
>
> **Do data-based decisions depersonalize decision making?** It's easy to sit back in an office reviewing data and handing out decisions, but what of the *people* responsible for inputting the information? What is their reasoning as to why the information shows what it does—good or otherwise? What would they suggest we focus our attention on in order to improve performance in the business?

When it comes to considering engaging with employees, customers, and other external sources to the business, it's the latter question that should cause you the greatest concern. The more CEOs and executives resort to using data to make decisions, the less likely we are to discuss, review, and collaborate with others to understand what specifically the data is telling us. How many times, for example, have you heard employees say that the "system" forces them to take shortcuts or enter data in an unusual fashion? My guess is that you've heard this at your company and also while interacting with others including at retail malls, and automotive dealerships, and even while speaking with customer help desks over the phone. These comments are signs that an appetite for data from the C-suite drives employees to modify information to identify the desired outcome. So what good is the data if it's being manipulated?

If Coca-Cola had asked a large cross-section of its employees and customers whether they believed a reformulation and rebranding of Coke was a good idea, rather than relying on market research and keeping the new brand under wraps, New Coke would likely never have existed, or at least would have been produced and introduced significantly differently than it was, and millions of dollars in research and advertising would have been saved (not to mention protection of Coke's brand).

If Netflix had engaged with employees and customers on its pending decision to split the DVD and streaming businesses with the creation of Qwikster, it likely would not have made the decision to do so, salvaging its brand and millions of dollars.

Data is a tool that provides measurement and validation. It's true that we need measurement in order to assess progress and understand what's working well and what's not, but this shouldn't distract us from interacting with those responsible for creating the data in the first place in order to understand the accuracy and relevance of the data that is being provided.

When it comes to managing the implementation of a strategy, the capturing and measurement of data provides a means by which to *validate* progress, recognize potential obstacles, and identify hidden opportunities. That's it. These outcomes, however, can't be achieved without applying the SURE model for implementation of the desired measurements: SURE stands for measurements that are Simple to comprehend, Understood by everyone, Realistically achievable, and can be Extemporaneously accomplished. Measures that align with the SURE method can only be developed through the involvement of and collaboration with employees that in turn increases employees' alignment, commitment, and accountability. Are you recognizing a trend here?

A Multilevel Approach to Strategic Measurement Formulation

With all of these discussions about measurements, you may begin to wonder, when and how can measurements be incorporated at all? The approach I recommend to clients and to you is to incorporate collaborative measures at four separate stages of the strategy formulation process:

1. **Vision.** What will the company look like when we achieve the vision?
2. **Strategic objectives.** What will successful achievement of the objective result in?

3. **Strategic string.** How will achievement of the strategic string result in supporting the strategic objective?
4. **Actions.** What will the successful completion of the action look like?

Here is an example of multilevel strategic measurements, taken from the strategy of a large international flooring distributor whom I worked with recently:

> **Vision.** We bring unique flooring products at competitive prices to customers across North America, helping them build and create homes that ignite passion and excitement. *Measure: Capture 50 percent of the North American market in sales of unique stone flooring products.*
>
> **Strategic objective #1.** Build a recognizable brand presence in North America. *Measure: Have a preferred relationship and pricing model in place in 40 percent of all major flooring distributors across North America.*
>
> **Strategic string #1 (for strategic objective #1).** Form business relationships with 75 percent of the key flooring distributors in North America that we want to partner with. *Measure: Pricing lists and samples sent following initial contact to 75 percent of major flooring distributors in North America.*
>
> **Action #1 (for strategic string #1).** Identify all major flooring distributors in North America. *Measure: List of flooring distributors, including company name, address, and president contact information complete.*

Notice in this example that each level supports the achievement of the previous level, and that each measure aligns with the SURE model. What you might also notice is that the measures selected by the flooring distributor represent meaning to the company. For example, you may believe that capturing 50 percent of the North American market isn't sufficient to achieve the vision, and that would be fine if this were your own strategy. These measures were selected by the flooring distributor in conjunction with its employees to ensure that both the actions and the measures were *reasonably achievable.*

To formulate measures that align with the SURE model, consider any one or a combination of the following questions:

> *What does success look like in this instance?*
>
> *How will we recognize the objective when we reach it?*
>
> *What will change as a result of reaching this objective?*
>
> *How will this objective improve our business?*
>
> *What is the key measure that will identify to everyone that we have achieved our objective?*

For a more detailed overview of how to create a strategy incorporating the SURE model of measurement development, as well as dozens of other resources to help empower your operation, visit www.operational empowerment.com.

You might also be wondering at this point who should be involved in formulating actions at each of these levels, as it is clearly unrealistic to involve every single stakeholder or employee. It's unrealistic to believe that you can involve everyone, nor should you attempt to do so. The key is to align stakeholders based on their understanding of, and ability to contribute to, the strategy. Identifying key stakeholders for each area of the strategy begins by considering the following groups:

> **Vision stakeholders** include customers, employees, board members, and senior management.
>
> **Strategic objective and strategic string stakeholders** include board members, senior management, middle management, and employees.
>
> **Action plan stakeholders** are limited to middle management, frontline supervisors, and employees.

Notice that employees are engaged in each level of strategic measurement formulation. This ensures their continued engagement in the strategy as it is fully formulated, which in turn maximizes their involvement and interest in how the strategy will progress and roll out. As I've alluded to several times in this chapter, the earlier and more frequently you can involve employees in the strategy formulation and planning process, the better your chances at achieving the strategy.

With key stakeholder groups identified, the next and final step is to select the most appropriate individuals that represent each stakeholder group well. I consider this approach to be part art and part science, with a slight bit of luck. I typically make these selections with my clients by progressing through the following steps:

1. Ask for volunteers within each stakeholder group.
2. Ask other stakeholders whom they would recommend to be part of the process.
3. Seek out those who have the knowledge and/or respect of others within their peer group.

If too many stakeholders are identified, I use a process of elimination by working backward through the list above, selecting first those who have the knowledge and/or respect of their peers, then filling remaining voids with those who were recommended to be part of the process, then using any remaining volunteers. You might notice that this approach may leave out some volunteers; however, remember that this is only if I have too many stakeholders—which is rare. Most times few volunteer, and I use this as a starting point to build momentum (people want to join a team when they see others are already there and participating; refer back to my earlier discussions in Chapter 3 about building a community). If I have volunteers remaining, I engage them in other parts of the strategy action planning and communication process.

Why Your Strategy Ain't Jack

Even the fastest cars and motorcycles require constant tuning to maximize their speed and reliability. The best mechanics never settle with "good enough"—they are always seeking to find additional horsepower to give their driver or rider a competitive advantage. The same theory applies in strategy. This isn't a plan to be poured in concrete or placed behind glass. Strategy is a road map, and like any road it will be filled with bumps, detours, and roadblocks. It's not as important to follow the plan as it is to remain focused on the vision, though remaining focused in this manner requires an ability to adjust and change course as necessary. Like the old saying that goes, "Jack be nimble, Jack be quick," a strategy must retain a foothold in reality as well as the ability to be dynamic, changing course when unexpected or unplanned forces exist. To ensure the strategy is dynamic, I recommend many of my clients to perform an annual strategy review as a means of ensuring consistent focus on direction while allowing for dynamic shifts in objectives and actions.

I'm not suggesting you book another retreat off-site for several days, but a rapid strategy review with key stakeholders in order to assess progress and ensure relevance. When I do these reviews for clients, we typically review the following aspects of the strategy:

> **Customer needs.** What demands have our customers made or requested since our last review? Considerations include customer feedback, shifts in product or service demands, and prospective customer intelligence.
>
> **Market dynamics.** What has been realized or changed in the market since our last review? Considerations include new product developments, shifting demographics, and economic factors.
>
> **Competitive influences.** What has changed in the competitive landscape? Considerations include new competitors in the market, new competitor products or services, and shifts in pricing and value perceptions.
>
> **Workforce dynamics.** What has changed in the dynamics of our workforce? Considerations include employee attrition rates, retention, training and development needs, and skill gaps based on changes in any of the areas outlined above.

By performing a 12-month or even a 6-month review of your strategy, you are well positioned to make adjustments in enough time to respond to shifts that may derail or influence your ability to achieve the vision. Similar to the formulation of the strategy, being successful hinges on obtaining critical inputs, ideas, and intelligence from employees, as well as ensuring their active participation in the process.

A strategy is not a secret document to be formulated in isolation. It is a road map to the future vision of the organization, and in order to succeed it must involve employees at every stage of formulation and development and implementation. By building a strategy in this manner, you create a strong connection between what employees are working toward and what you want to achieve.

5

Engage the Masses

Building a Continuous Improvement Community

At the risk of dating myself, I can still vividly recall visiting my dad's office during the early 1980s. As a public accountant for a local utility, my father was fortunate to work with one of the first computers purchased in our area. Compared to the computers of today, I think it's fair to describe the monstrosity as a room full of equipment rather than a computer. I recall how enthusiastic my dad was to have one; and he was overjoyed at the ability of the massive machine to make calculations and print out statements and reports that he would otherwise have had to create by hand. The advent of computers was something that my dad will never forget, and as his needs and capabilities to manipulate reports and outputs from the computer evolved, so did the technology. Dad was (and still is) an advocate of continuous improvement, having taken the lead during his career in introducing several hardware and software upgrades at the utility. He became a self-taught student of technology, recognizing that improvement comes only if pursued, and as his role evolved into managing others, he focused on instilling this same philosophy in those he led.

Relative to empowering business operations, there are a few critical points that one can derive from my father's journey:

- There are specific events that occurred during my father's career that influenced how he perceived the business and its ability to best serve its customers.
- These events and changes influenced my father's thoughts, beliefs, and actions.
- To continue to best serve customers, my father recognized the necessity of continuously pursuing improvement, engaging others around him in the pursuit.

Reflect for a moment on the changes that have occurred during your grandparents' lives, your parents' lives, and your life. All these changes have influenced how each generation lives, thinks, and acts. How we live, think, and act in turn translates into how we interact in our work environment, regardless of our title, position, or industry. Consider, for example, that our demand today for instantaneous information, our diminishing attention span, the influence of the Internet, heightened global security measures, fashion, food safety, and globalization have all had a significant impact on how our businesses operate because they have affected those within the organization based on their generation and their life experiences. Here are a few examples that demonstrate the influence of these life events:

- The introduction of services like iTunes has diminished the brick-and-mortar businesses of companies like HMV.
- Video streaming has supported the massive growth of companies such as Netflix, while demolishing Blockbuster virtually overnight.
- The rising cost of postsecondary education has nurtured the growth of online education providers such as the University of Phoenix.
- The advent of services such as Google and Bing has virtually eliminated the sale of encyclopedias.
- Increasing developments in electric motors and battery life are influencing consumer acceptance of hybrid and electric vehicles as a primary form of transportation.

- The growth in popularity of online forums and communities has diminished association member demands for face-to-face networking events.
- The ability to pay bills and share data online with services such as PayPal and Dropbox have dramatically reduced the revenue and impacted the business model of postal and courier services.

These are just a few examples of the influence that life events and evolution have had on business, and they bring about an important realization. If vision and strategy act as a road map for a business, then we must form within each business a community that is focused on continuous evolution and improvement if we are to ensure that we can adapt to and act upon the changes occurring outside of the business that influence both customers and employees in how they think, act, and respond.

Continuous improvement is not an opportunity, but a necessity to ensure survival. We can no longer remain stagnant with the same mindset as yesterday. CEOs, executives, managers, and employees must come together as a community to elevate their combined level of thinking through collaboration, improve their ability to introduce and capitalize on innovation, and seek to obtain constant and never-ending improvement.

These are the three pillars to business improvement (Figure 5.1).

FIGURE 5.1 Three Pillars of Business Improvement

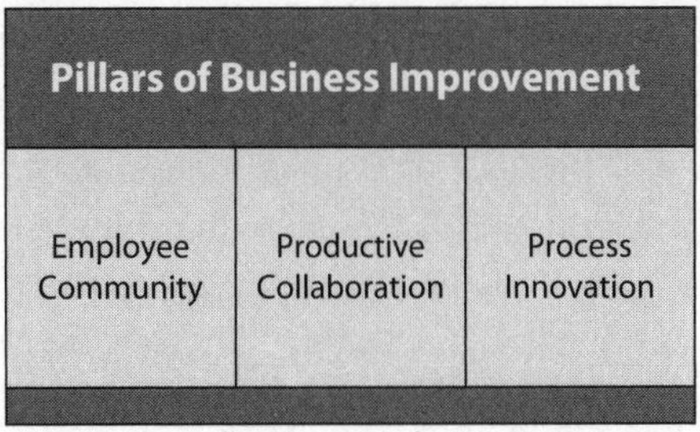

Pillars of Business Improvement		
Employee Community	Productive Collaboration	Process Innovation

Continuous improvement requires our adaptability and response to change, yet statistics originally presented by John Kotter in 1995[1] and later validated by McKinsey[2] suggest that our rate of success in introducing and sustaining large-scale corporate change is a meager 30 percent. This suggests that our ability to sustain the "continuous" portion of the continuous improvement equation is less than stellar, at a time when introducing and sustaining change is crucial to survival. This invites the question, how can we sustain the "continuous" in improvement?

Why Most Improvements Fail to Be Continuous, and What You Can Do About It

As I am writing this, I have returned from a meeting with a prospective client who after several conversations asked for my help. It seems that after decades of operating a thriving automotive manufacturing facility, offshore competition and downward pressure on pricing, coupled with steadily increasing overhead, have diminished profit margins and ultimately threatened the survival of the business. The owner had spent much of his career building up the family-owned business, and more recently was fighting to sustain it, but with his son now involved, he feels the need to effect significant improvement in their operations before officially turning over the reins to his son. The owner wants to pass on a business that is "set" to survive the next 10 to 20 years, allowing his son the chance at sustaining success just as he has.

The challenge that the father and son are experiencing is an increasing demand for customization of products, with diminishing volume. This challenges a factory that has been set up to handle large-scale batch processing and in turn creates significant issues for the continuation of a thriving business, not the least of which include excessive amounts of inventory, late customer deliveries, and an inability to effectively estimate the costs associated with overhead and profitability. After several initial discussions, I spent time with the operations and manufacturing managers to better understand what they believed were the greatest challenges the business was facing. Their feedback was something I have heard all too often. Over the years, as a result of cutbacks in staffing (as volumes diminished) along with the introduction of new technology, there had been a reduction in the amount of information and "visibility" the shop floor was receiving. They were unable to effectively capitalize on machine efficiencies and operator talents as order lot sizes diminished, resulting in longer than normal lead times. In addition, their ability historically to see orders several weeks in advance had allowed them to produce WIP as needed. However, the diminished visibility meant that WIP levels were unstable, which resulted in fits and spurts of production to attempt to meet demand.

Several ideas and improvements had been introduced along the way, from a whiteboard for greater visibility of order status on the shop floor, to daily production meetings to increase communication between sales and production, to a review of WIP inventory minimum and maximum levels, but unfortunately the hectic pace of work and lack of available time had resulted in these initiatives being abandoned. The improvements had not been given sufficient time to take hold, nor had they been treated as a priority; therefore they hadn't brought about any of the desired results.

Through discussions with the owner and his son it became apparent that their view was that the previous improvements had not helped in any manner. "We tried those things, but they didn't help. What other ideas do you have?"

And there it is: the number one reason why improvement fails to be continuous. An idea is introduced, albeit often insufficiently and with little planning; it survives for a week, possibly even a month, then suffers a quick and painful death, leaving behind the belief of those involved that "We tried that; it didn't work." Heaven forbid that you try to introduce a similar idea in the future, because the idea is forever labeled as, "We tried that; it didn't work."

Improvement isn't static; it's an evolution. If you look up the definition of *improvement*, you will find synonyms such as *development*, *refinement*, and *advancement*. Notice that all of these words suggest progression, not a specific point in time. We need to realize that improvement in and of itself must be continuous if we are going to realize any significant benefits. "Tried that; didn't work; went back to the way we used to do it," is not improvement—it is the definition of operational insanity. Improving operational performance is often more an evolution, than a revolution, supporting why most initiatives are left to gather dust rather than seen through to fruition.

To ensure that improvement is continuous, we need to invest more time in effectively planning and preparing for the improvement by specifically addressing the following:

1. **Engage the collaboration of many.** There is no such thing as the *power of one* when it comes to introducing and instituting improvements; success and sustainability come from the *collaboration of many*. Ideas for process or product improvements, for example, should be generated in groups, not simply by one or two people and especially not solely by those in management. It's through the *collaboration of many* that we prompt new and innovative ideas, build numerous champions in support of the initiative, and create a broad commitment to initiating the improvement.

2. **Consider idea iterations.** The fastest way to derail any improvement idea is to fail to consider how the idea might evolve. McDonald's has been selling coffee for years, without much consideration for how the product might evolve and how it might capitalize on a growing market for quick-serve coffee. It didn't wake up to the idea until companies such as Dunkin' Donuts and Starbucks began selling breakfast food (the real reason McDonald's sold coffee in the first place). Then new iterations were formulated through the introduction of McCafé, and McDonald's success in the coffee market began to grow. Every improvement to a process, product, or service must be considered for how it will evolve in order to ensure plans are in place to move the improvement forward on a continuum.

3. **Accept prudent risk.** For every new product or service that is introduced, there are plenty of risks. For every change in process that is introduced, there are also plenty of risks. This does not mean that we should turn ideation processes over to those in the risk management group for an ongoing assessment. Where there is no risk, there is also no reward. Identify potential risks, qualify them for the impact they may have, and then identify contingent and

preventative measures. With this in place there should be nothing stopping your progress forward.

4. **Set checkpoints for continuity.** In downhill slalom ski racing there are several checkpoints along the route, allowing for time checks and feedback on angles and positioning on the hill. It's through these checkpoints that progress can be measured. If times are slower at a gate than previously, there must be a reason. When pursuing improvement, checkpoints or quality gates must be put into place, otherwise there is no way to clearly measure if we are in fact improving (see Chapter 4 for ideas on how to create better measures using the SURE method). These can be as simple as follow-up meetings with the key stakeholders involved or more complex measures that allow for monitoring. Either way, without checkpoints there is no way to ensure continuity of the change.

5. **Capitalize on momentum.** In any change initiative, it's common to focus on low-hanging fruit first—where can we achieve the biggest bang for our buck without investing significant time or energy? This approach creates momentum that allows for larger or more complex issues to be tackled while positive energy and confidence are high. To ensure that improvement is continuous, it is critical to consider where we are going next. How will the momentum obtained through the success of the initial improvement be used to tackle other areas or opportunities within the business?

To put the *continuous* in improvement therefore requires collaboratively looking forward to best ascertain opportunities and risks through ideation while planning for continuity, all with the intent of building momentum to maximize the value of outcomes and gain support for sustaining the improvement.

From Culture to Community: Forming a Platform of Perpetual Improvement

Since the adoption of continuous improvement principles and practices into North America dating back to the Second World War,[3] the general focus has been to instill or cement continuous improvement into organizational culture. The challenge has been that within each organizational culture there exist several distinct subcultures (a concept I discussed earlier in Chapter 4), hence shifting a cultural mindset to focus on improvement is ineffective if you aren't able to combine collaborative teams of like-minded individuals—or communities. This is where the concept of building a continuous improvement community comes into play.

A community is a subset of a culture, formed on the basis of like-minded individuals who have similar interests, similar goals, and complementary skills and abilities (Figure 5.2). A hockey team is a great example of a small community. All of the players, despite varying positions and roles, have a single objective in mind—to win! In order to win, not only do they need to constantly improve their individual skills, but through training and practice they must learn to identify their collective strengths and weaknesses, allowing them to work as a team to constantly improve their performance. This may come in the form of changing positions or changing players, but the nucleus of the team never changes. Surrounding the team is a community of support, including coaches and trainers. There is also a community of people, the fans, who come together and support the team. Each surrounding community plays a different role, but collectively they have the same objective.

FIGURE 5.2 Community of Support

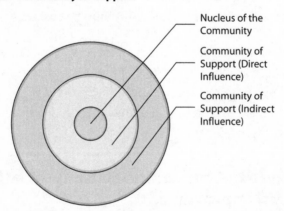

Nucleus of the Community

Community of Support (Direct Influence)

Community of Support (Indirect Influence)

It's through the power of a community that we experience an evolution in performance on a continuum. A strong hockey team with a bad coach or trainer will likely not reach its full potential, however the strength of the community of team players will likely result in the ousting of the coach or trainer. By forming communities, we create a perpetual cycle of improvement in performance as the group constantly strives to naturally remove barriers and obstacles while steadily improving performance.

I used Wikipedia recently and was prompted to make a small donation in order to support the Wikipedia community. What a worthwhile cause based on the value Wikipedia provides. In fact, Wikipedia is built upon a community of improvement. The content is written collaboratively by the people who use it. Does everyone contribute to Wikipedia? No. However, anyone who chooses to join the wiki community can sign in and make improvements to content. This is the basis for creating a platform of perpetual improvement, as there will always be someone, somewhere, with new or additional information that will contribute to the accuracy and relevance of what Wikipedia communicates. When Wikipedia was designed, the builders did not seek to force others to conform to the builders' needs (for an example of organizations that have tried this approach, look no further than the earliest iterations of the website www.healthcare.gov); instead they built a platform that encouraged and made it easy for those interested to participate. In doing so they created an attraction to the community of like-minded individuals, and through the ease of platform use they have ensured an ongoing array of improvements to the online content that will always yield improved results.

In fact, Wikipedia's model is more than just a user-friendly collaborative platform that facilitates continuous improvement. In the early 1990s, Microsoft purchased exclusive rights to Funk and Wagnall's encyclopedias, providing Microsoft with the articles, photos, and other resources necessary to produce a software called Encarta.[4] Encarta was developed to compete with *Compton's Multimedia Encyclopedia* and *The New Grolier Multimedia Encyclopedia*, which were quickly gaining market share over previous print encyclopedias such as *Encyclopedia Britannica*. Despite an initial success in sales, the Encarta software platform was shut down in late 2009 after the rapid growth of free online encyclopedias, such as Wikipedia, made the purchase of encyclopedia software obsolete. The community-based platform that Wikipedia offered actually quashed out Microsoft's Encarta platform, as it offered free access to a community-based platform that remained current as a result of continuous contributions and improvements made by users.

There are dozens of other organizations that have recognized the power of communities in support of continuous improvement; here are a few examples of companies that have been built upon a community platform that facilitates ongoing improvement:

- TripAdvisor LLC is a community built upon user reviews of travel-related content.
- eBay facilitates B2B and C2C sales in a community.
- Sony PlayStation operates in a community of users facilitating online gaming and sharing.
- Facebook is a community that provides real-time news, reviews, and other resources.

You'll notice in reflecting on the success of each of these communities that there are distinct similarities:

- They all offer the ability for users to choose whether they want to participate or not.
- They ensure that information is shared in real time.
- They are self-governing.
- There are no leaders or individuals who "manage."
- They ensure transparency in information sharing.
- There are limited filters allowing community participants to share freely.
- They continue to evolve and improve as users contribute and suggest changes.
- Those outside of the community are drawn to it based on the appeal of participation.

Rather than focusing on shifting, improving, or worse yet managing our cultures, we need to build, nurture, and support the development of communities. It is through communities that we can facilitate ongoing improvement. In doing so, we have to first let go of our desire to "manage" others; in a community, those who are in leadership roles actually focus their energy and efforts on providing support to the community, rather than managing it. Building a community of continuous improvement requires a shift from managing people to empowering people, specifically in:

- Providing the tools and resources to support the self-sustainment of the community.
- Empowering those within the community to make decisions that affect their desired outcomes.
- Empowering community members to take action and resolve challenges.
- Facilitating open communication and sharing of information across the community.
- Empowering the community to self-govern, removing those who aren't contributing.

Specific to a continuous improvement community, before we discuss how to create one I want you to ponder something. Making a shift to a community of improvement, rather than focusing on reeducating and changing a culture, threatens everything we have understood and adopted up to now. It is, in essence, turning the hierarchy of management upside down, and moving power from those who manage to those who participate. This is not an easy shift to make; it is the very reason that "employee empowerment" has not been widely received or adapted well into the corporate world. Let's be honest, not too many executives or managers want to turn over power to their employees, particularly when it comes to introducing changes and improvements to the organization that may impact the role, responsibility, or priorities of management. However, when you consider the power of communities I mentioned earlier, *and* you realize that as human beings we are all being influenced by the communities that exist (influencing our desire for more active participation and decision making and less management by others), then the choice is not whether we form communities, it's when. If we delay the decision for much longer, we will see decreasing employee engagement and employee retention.

Wait a minute—aren't we experiencing this already?

Build Your Own Continuous Improvement Community

For several years, my client Mike Vokes of Vokes Furniture had struggled with finding and hiring the right plant manager. Candidates, although technically competent, all had a difficult time fitting into the business. There appeared to be a variety of contributing factors, but after the third plant manager didn't work out, Mike dreaded the idea of hiring yet another one who was likely to have a steep learning curve, with little chance of fitting into the Vokes Furniture community.

Mike took it upon himself to reconsider his need for a plant manager. His vision for the company was to have employees take responsibility and make decisions on their own, minimizing downtime and increasing the empowerment and morale of the staff. Before heading down the same path of seeking yet another plant manager, he met with some key employees to ask what they thought was missing. The feedback was overwhelmingly similar—in essence the employees felt that there was nothing a plant manager could bring to the table that they couldn't already handle themselves. All that was necessary was the ability to make decisions, as waiting on Mike, who often traveled to visit with customers and other industry partners, caused unnecessary delays and frustration.

Mike decided to pilot a small project in which we worked together to select four key team members, all having expertise in their functional area, who had the ability to make decisions on their own and were respected by the other members of their area, and made them team leaders. After meeting with the team leaders to discuss his intent, he pulled all of the employees together to discuss the idea with them, asking for their input. Once again feedback was unanimous—there was an overwhelming majority of employees who wanted to try the new approach in favor of bringing in yet another outsider who didn't understand the business.

It was at this point that Mike and I began working together on a project to introduce the new team leader approach and in turn reduce his time spent in managing day-to-day operations, shifting greater responsibility to the new team leaders. After reviewing the current model and initial successes, several things became apparent. Team leaders wanted:

1. Greater responsibility to make decisions that impacted their functional area
2. More communication from Mike and with each other to better understand the business and its daily operations
3. Additional opportunities to delegate management of floor operations to the team leaders (such as inventory management)

The team leaders as a group were becoming increasingly collaborative, sharing information and offering support to one another in order to facilitate improved work flow.

When we first connected, Mike was still unsure as to whether a plant manager would improve the operation and free him from some of the tactical operational activities, but as we continued to empower the team leaders and focus on building their knowledge, inter-team communication, and their ability to manage all aspects of their functional areas, his confidence in the team leader model (and the confidence of the team leaders themselves) grew.

I share this example because it aligns with several key points we have been discussing up until this point, namely:

- Forming a community of like-minded individuals serves to create a perpetual succession of improvement.
- Once a community is formed, it becomes self-managing, shunning ideas, individuals, or circumstances that don't lead or support its cause.

- Empowering employees who exist within a community increases their desire for increasing responsibility and empowerment.
- A community will evolve through support, diminishing the need to manage those within it.

The following steps are necessary to form a continuous improvement community such as the one at Vokes Furniture.

A Continuous Improvement Community Must Have Conviction

For a community to exist there must be a modus operandi that serves to appeal to, attract, and connect the members of the community. In the case of Vokes Furniture the community formed for several reasons:

- Perceived pain and discomfort in welcoming and adapting to a new plant manager.
- The belief that the president had the best interest of the employees at heart.
- A demonstration of commitment to employees by giving trust and empowerment.

A Community Hinges on Equal Opportunity for Involvement

This past year served as an election year for national party leaders in the small community I live in. The national party leader in my community was unanimously voted in; however, several other party leaders in other areas across the region were not. Being voted into power, or not, is a clear signal as to the community's belief in the direction and support offered by the political leader. A community that allows participants to select their own champions and leaders increases the community's commitment to the leaders. This is counterintuitive to the way many corporate and business leaders are selected today, often a practice of leaders identifying other leaders, most often with minimal input (if any) from the employees that will be led. To build a community of continuous improvement requires an equal opportunity for employees to be involved and act as a leader (formally or informally) for the group.

Communication Is the Collaborative Vehicle to Facilitate a Community
A community is able to improve only if members can rapidly identify and resolve challenges and pursue opportunities. For members of the community to make decisions and rally in support of pursuing and tackling challenges and opportunities, there must be dexterous communications and open dialogue. In the instance of Vokes Furniture, we improved the candidness, frequency, and value of communications. Communications contained three levels of relevance:

1. **External communications.** What's happening with customers, the market, and the community as it pertains to the business. This included new customer opportunities, customer concerns about quality and pricing, new competition, and other external factors.
2. **Internal communications.** What challenges and opportunities exist relative to how the business is operating today. This includes discussions of work flow, equipment, resources, and staffing in order to facilitate delivery of products and services.
3. **Functional communications.** What are the specific challenges, opportunities, or ideas relative to performance within each business unit or department. Discussion points can include equipment functionality, resources, and work flow all specific to each work unit.

Leadership Must Shift to a Supportive Rather Than a Prescriptive Role
Following our work together and during a review of the success of his community model, one of the greatest features that Mike spoke of was the shift in *his* role. Previously having stepped up to fill the vacant plant manager role, Mike had been spending considerable time interacting with and managing the tasks occurring on the shop floor. In the community model, Mike spent very little time on the production floor other than to obtain information from the team leaders. In fact, through the institution of twice-daily meetings Mike found that he began to obtain increased feedback from the team leaders as to what was necessary to

help them be successful, shifting his role from prescribing what each group should be doing to providing the necessary support and facilitation to assist the teams in being successful.

Building a continuous improvement community requires a shift in how operational and business leaders approach engaging, communicating with, and empowering their employees. With the right approach in place, a community will evolve and become self-managing and self-fulfilling, increasing the demands on leadership for further support and empowerment, thus creating a cycle of perpetual improvement that evolves with the support and nurturing of business leaders.

A Community Sustains Continuous Forever

Professional and trade associations are some of the longest-standing communities in existence today. The earliest association on record in the United States was the Chamber of Commerce of the State of New York, which was formed in 1768 by 20 merchants; it remains in existence today.[5]

Associations have evolved over time. Originally providing a foundation for cooperation of competition, today associations offer education, lobbying, and various other resources to their members. Associations that are in tune with and adapting to the progressive needs of their communities continue to thrive; those associations that fail to offer steadily increasing value to their members are struggling.

Several years ago I worked with the board of a small regional association. The board was struggling to cover base costs, most of which were split between administration (labor, overhead) and marketing costs (conferences, networking events, technology). At the board level, directors rarely dug into details other than listening to the presentations of association managers, but the predominant challenge they faced was how to stop the decline of revenue. Membership numbers remained relatively consistent year after year; however, participation in events had diminished. With a combination of baby boomers, generation X, and millennials amid the membership, there existed a diversity of opinions from members as to what they actually wanted to see the association provide them:

- There was a desire for increased networking events, but the association was consistently unable to attract enough members to attend networking events to cover base costs.
- There was a desire for online educational products, but the costs to convert materials to online media outweighed the revenue that would be achieved through their delivery (a significantly long ROI).
- Shelf life for educational materials was not significant enough to achieve a reasonable ROI from their development.
- The association was unable to estimate the costs and benefits of shifting to an online community that allowed for members to collaborate.

So what did they focus on? They did what many other associations choose to do: cut costs by reducing staff. This extended the use of outdated training materials and led to the creation of Mickey Mouse online solutions that were not user-friendly, all while continuing to market and offer the same solutions and format they always had—which continued to fuel revenue decline. The impact on membership retention and revenue was, not surprisingly, deleterious. Because they didn't respond to the various needs of member segments within the community due to fear of increasing costs in a declining revenue market, they in turn continued to drive a greater wedge between what the association offered and what the members desired.

The board was simply not a SMART board (Figure 5.3). It was unable to collaborate and innovate collectively to make strategic decisions and investments to support the evolving needs of the members. With 60 percent of the board being longstanding members from the baby boomer generation, there was always a majority vote to "do what we've always done."

FIGURE 5.3 SMART Board

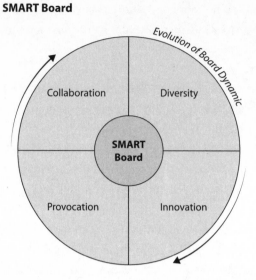

The board was not in tune with the needs of its community; it was not introducing improvements and changes that supported the community's evolving needs, and it was not empowering members of the community to become involved in the changes themselves. These are at the core of building and sustaining a community. These challenges can also be found in the corporate world today. When boards of corporations and senior leadership teams fail to understand what their employees want and need to be effective in their roles, choosing instead to initiate changes that they *believe* employees need, they are in effect moving away from building a community, deconstructing any that may already have existed, and instead attempting to form a management culture that suits their norms.

As discussed previously in this chapter, a community constructed and supported correctly will evolve naturally with the proper elements of conviction, involvement, communication, and supportive leadership in place. As the community evolves, however, it's crucial to recognize that the needs and demands of the community itself will change. This in turn requires that leaders find new ways to support the evolving levels of conviction, to enhance involvement by those within the community, and to use and introduce differing forms of communication in order to support the community evolution. Failure to support the evolution of the community results in a failed community.

When Ron Johnson attempted to transform JC Penney from a low-cost discount provider of clothing into an upscale retailer, one of his first moves was to make massive job cuts to restructure the company and cut costs. In addition to terminating the jobs of thousands of employees, Johnson also terminated many of his key executives. Presumably those who disagreed with his vision went first. After only 16 months at the helm of the once-dominant retailer, the CEO was terminated after long-time JC Penney customers left in droves, resulting in a near 25 percent drop in share value.[6]

What's interesting in this example is that Johnson's initial ambitions, to turn JC Penney from a low-cost discount provider to that of an upscale retailer, may not have been a bad idea, but how he went about doing so, in effect the impact he had on the JC Penney community by terminating hundreds of employees, was completely contradictory to what we've been discussing. Johnson in effect destroyed any sense of community that did exist at JC Penney in the name of forming a new community. He lacked patience for evolving the community, presumably due to pressure from the board to rapidly increase profitability. Thus rather than nurturing and supporting the evolution of the community, he destroyed it, along with employee morale, productivity, and profits (and customers).

Sustaining a community therefore requires that we:

1. **Recognize the current state of the community.** Is there a community in place today, and what is the direction of the community? What is the strength of the current community?
2. **Interact with the community.** Become a member of the community, rather than a leader. What do members of the community need in order to evolve and speed up their evolution in support of improvement?
3. **Segment and support.** What are the differing segments of the community today, and how might these segments be supported to improve the entire community as a whole (Figure 5.4)?

FIGURE 5.4 Community Segments and Support Mechanisms

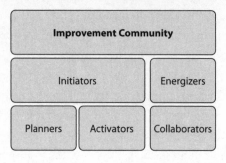

Improvement will become continuous if it is nurtured within a community, but in order to ensure continued improvement the community itself must first be nurtured. By focusing on the elements of supporting the sustainment and evolution of a community, we can in turn support ongoing improvement. This leaves us with the question of speed and urgency—after all, we can't just sit around and wait for a community to evolve. Similar to Ron Johnson's mission at JC Penney, time is often of the essence. This brings us to Chapter 6, where we will discuss how to increase velocity for results.

6

Hit the Ground Running

How to Increase Velocity for Rapid Results

Newton's First Law of Motion suggests that an object at rest stays at rest and an object in motion stays in motion with the same speed and in the same direction unless acted upon by an unbalanced force. Motion is the act or process of moving or being moved, and within every business motion exists. In any business, motion is facilitated through the processes, technology, equipment, and resources that are made available to employees in order to produce products and deliver services. The faster the motion, the faster employees are able to produce products or deliver their services, and in essence the faster a business can collect revenue and produce profits.

There is then a balance in finding the right motion in order to deliver products or services at an optimum speed that supports profitability. If, for instance, motion is increased to the point that the quality of the products or services is poor in the eyes of the customer, then sales and profitability decline as perceived value diminishes. I call this *excessive motion*. If, on the other hand, the motion is too slow, then products or services are not produced or delivered in a fashion to meet with customer demands, resulting in (once again) a lack of perceived value and diminishing sales and revenue. I call this *insufficient motion*. There is then an optimum level of motion that must be sustained if products and services are to align with customer demands (Figure 6.1). It's not enough to find the optimum motion, but we must have the ability to govern the speed of motion by increasing it or decreasing it in order to meet ever-evolving customer needs. This is the equilibrium of motion.

FIGURE 6.1   Balancing Market Motion

In a business it stands to reason that motion is generated by employees. Let's take a moment to let this sink in. Motion is not created by technology, equipment, or other resources; it is generated by people. Resources and tools such as technology are meant to facilitate motion, but they do not create it. Consider that an automated service such as what you might experience when calling a bank to complete transactions over the phone was developed by people. The developers decided how fast the attendant should speak and what options would be made available to the customer. In fact, it was a person or a group of people who made the decision to incorporate the automated calling feature for the bank in the first place. You might have the best technology or equipment that money can buy, but without people you will be unable to fully capitalize on your investment.

Motion is therefore controlled by an employee's ability to act, and the greater the obstacles to taking action, the slower the employee's ability to generate motion. Put another way, it's not enough to facilitate motion; we have to create and initiate motion that is aligned in both speed and direction in order to facilitate the natural building of momentum and progress. Any barriers or obstacles that influence an employee's ability to act result in motion being sped up, slowed down, or misdirected, all of which reduce momentum.

If you've ever been to a sporting event, then you've experienced the type of motion I'm referring to when you tried to leave the stadium. Once the game ends, the majority of fans head for the exits, but they do so at differing speeds. Some people stop at the washroom before they leave, others stop to talk to friends, and some wander aimlessly in search of an exit that will bring them closest to where they parked. There are multiple forms of motion at play. Those who virtually run over other people to exit the stadium are applying excessive motion, often impacting the ability of others to move toward the exit and making enemies along the way; those who practice insufficient motion slow down anyone who ends up following their lead. If the speed and direction of fans leaving the building could be optimized toward the closest exit, then motion would be optimized and momentum would *naturally* build.

Watching the flow of traffic on a congested highway is another way to witness the power of optimized motion. Highways are designed to allow slower cars and trucks to move to the right, while drivers who desire to move quickly drive past them in the left lane. Several years ago my father travelled through Montana and noticed that his speed (although just under the speed limit) was considerably slower than the traffic that was passing him. As a result, he increased his speed to match that of the majority of traffic. He optimized his speed, already heading in the same direction, which resulted in reaching his destination sooner. His momentum was naturally increased as a result of aligning his speed and direction with those around him.

Companies that empower their employees to improve their operations recognize the necessity to optimize the speed and direction of their employees in order to generate motion and create momentum.

So far we have discussed putting the foundation in place for performance, but now we need to identify how to best position these elements in order to facilitate momentum. In this chapter, we will discuss how to take the building blocks of an operational foundation, coupled with a collaborative strategy and supported by a continuous improvement community, and synchronize speed and direction to generate motion and momentum in order to achieve your desired results. After all, it's all about the results!

A Symphony Can Only Have One Director: Direction Facilitates Motion

I played the alto saxophone in music class throughout high school, taking classes well beyond the minimum credit requirements. I enjoyed playing in class despite my mediocre musical talents, but I owe my good grades to John. A musical genius, John was the only other alto saxophone player in my class. This meant that I sat next to John and shared music with him. John was naturally talented and could play a song effortlessly before I could clearly interpret the first verse. If I had trouble with a note, whether I knew it or not, John would provide me with feedback or coaching to help me get the note right. Being a visual person, I often found it difficult to read music for the first time and play it correctly. John, realizing this, would show me on his saxophone exactly what keys to hit in order to match the music.

As our music teacher, Mr. Taylor, would conduct, John and a handful of other star musicians in our class would assist others who struggled with the music, helping them to interpret and play at the correct pace and tone. The result was an orchestra of sound, facilitated by our conductor but learned through peer support.

I owe my ability to read music to Mr. Taylor, but I owe my ability to convert written music into recognizable sounds to John.

Passionate about music, Mr. Taylor conducted several small classes of 15 to 20 musicians, but he also headed several orchestras in the region, ranging from 50 to nearly 100 musicians, and the results were always the same: synchronized music. You might wonder how Mr. Taylor (or any other conductor for that matter) is able to keep such a large group of people, all with different instruments, different music, and different levels of experience, to produce such magnificent music. The secret is in how motion is created and aligned to produce harmony.

Similar to how John supported me, every orchestra contains those who are quick learners with the talent to read and interpret music, and the ability to help others do the same. Left to their own devices, these people will naturally support others around them, who in turn will seek them out, eager for additional support, all with the intent of producing harmony. An orchestra is designed to be led by one person, but supported by many. It is a community of like-minded people who have a vision to achieve harmony, and they will achieve harmony as long as the foundational building blocks of properly functioning instruments and easily interpreted music are in place.

Let's say, however, that you put a conductor in place who simply is not good at keeping tempo. What happens? The music, the harmony, and the morale of the group will fall apart. The number one role of a conductor is to keep the tempo, without which the entire symphony will fall apart. The tempo is the direction for the group. It allows all of the musicians (with instruments and instructions in hand) to know what they should be doing and when they should do it. They need not worry about what other musicians are playing or when they are playing it, all they need is a clear tempo and the results will be harmonious music.

To create motion that is poised for building momentum, there must first be direction. In a business, that direction is facilitated through policies, procedures, processes, and other work instructions. Just reading this list should provide insight into why direction is often not correct. Look around your company today for examples, and you are likely to find that:

- There is conflicting information between policies, procedures, and work instructions.
- Existing procedures or other work instructions are out-of-date and do not reflect current work practices.
- Not everyone is following procedures as intended, because they've found a better way to do them, yet have been unable to find the time or engage those who will update the procedure.
- Work instructions given by frontline leaders or managers often conflict with what procedures or past practices would suggest employees should do.

- Improperly functioning equipment necessitates performing processes other than as they were intended.
- Technology influences how people are completing work, making procedures seemingly unnecessary and inaccurate.

I could go on.

There seems to be a never-ending stream of reasons why our collective direction is not optimized, yet our preferred means of overcoming these weaknesses is to better manage our employees. Let me ask you, what do you think would have happened if Mr. Taylor had started picking out certain participants in the orchestra and giving them more direction? Would his instruction confuse others? Would it lead others to believe that they should rely solely on him for instruction, rather than learning from those around them?

The answer is yes. Identifying and incorporating the right direction to optimize our motion and increase momentum is not created through an increased focus on management but in fact by doing the opposite: empowering people to resolve the problems themselves. When I played with John in the band in high school and I was out of tune, John knew before Mr. Taylor or anyone else. Playing out of tune created confusion for those around me, so John naturally did what was necessary to correct me. Mr. Taylor often never even knew I was off key because other musicians were empowered to take action to rectify the situation. We naturally optimized our direction by supporting one another.

Refer back to my example of Vokes Furniture in the previous chapter. The president had, like so many other business owners, tried to introduce someone to "manage" the people in order to have everyone pursuing the same direction at the same time, but each and every time his attempts failed. His employees were rejecting being managed, which was evident in the minimal communication and diminishing performance of the group when a plant manager was put into place. It wasn't until the president selected a few of his strongest and most well-respected employees and made them team leaders, and transitioned himself from an employee-facing management role to a more distant and supportive conductor role, that his employees began performing at optimum levels. Their alignment and direction evolved quickly and naturally, with a steady increase in the productivity of the group as he focused efforts less on managing and more on providing support in the way of new tools, resources, information, and communication. Alignment of direction through the empowerment of employees took Vokes Furniture from an average-performing plant to an above-average-performing collaborative powerhouse.

When we study this approach, we can see that several aspects are critical in order to align the direction of the employees to create motion and in turn momentum:

1. **Empower people, not leadership.** Provide increased power to employees to identify, decide upon, and effect changes that are necessary to make their jobs easier and to increase productivity. Leadership power should be compartmentalized to making decisions and investing budget in support of employee needs and requests.

2. **Transition leaders from "manager" to "conductor."** Educate high-level leadership on the role of a conductor, remaining in sync with employee needs and helping employees make connections between employee needs and business objectives. The leader's role becomes keeping the tempo, while empowering and supporting employees in introducing changes that support their efforts.

3. **Diminish departments in favor of cross-functional teams.** Think less about building departments of like talent such as engineering and finance, and build team units that support different aspects of the business and its customers. A customer support team, for example, should include customer support representatives, information technologists, supplier contract managers, and sales representatives, all supported by a conductor of customer support.

4. **Empower employees to develop processes and procedures in collaborative teams.** Procedure or policy writing is not something that should be done in isolation if it is to remain current and engage those who are to apply the methods. By empowering the teams to write, revise, and retain their own policies and procedures, guiding documents become a method to support team

development (new hires, cross-functional training), and in turn are kept current and relevant, as doing anything less only serves to hinder the performance of the team and create frustration. With no one to point blame at for the frustration, processes tend to be updated more frequently.

5. **Introduce equipment and technology based on employee needs, not management incentives.** By forming cross-functional teams, ideas and recommendations for new software, equipment, or resources naturally become a team initiative rather than a department initiative. The introduction of new software, for example, is more likely to form out of a need identified by those within the team, and it is more likely to suit the needs of the team as fit or validation testing is done with team members as the primary customers rather than a secondary consideration.

It is by introducing changes in how various talents interact and align in support of the customer, all supported rather than managed by leadership, that we create alignment in a direction that evolves naturally to support momentum in motion.

But what if the natural momentum is simply not rapid enough to meet the needs of the customer? This is where *applied velocity* comes into play!

Become a Speed Freak: The Art and Science of Applied Velocity

If patience were a virtue, most businesses as we know them today would be defunct. The reality is that waiting for a team to align and strike its own rhythm may seem unrealistic. After all, you've got bills to pay, customers to please, and shareholders to satisfy. The bad news is that striking this rhythm does take some time, which can extend from months to even years. The faster the conductor works to ensure that the right team members are in place (those who have the right skills, fit within the community, and are collaborative), then the shorter the time span to achieve synchronicity. Once the team is aligned in a direction, however, the opportunity exists to turn up the dial and rapidly increase the productivity and results the team accomplishes.

Think of this like teaching a child to ride a bicycle for the first time. With my oldest son, Matthew, we began the process by purchasing him a bike with no pedals, otherwise known as a balance-bike. At the age of three he began by simply sitting on the bike, transitioning to walking while sitting on the bike, to eventually pushing himself down hills and gliding without touching the ground. With this mastered, he moved on to a bigger bicycle with pedals and training wheels at the age of four. Now comfortable with how to balance, and with training wheels in place, my son was able to focus solely on pedaling, building up strength and endurance during the process. By the age of five, we removed the training wheels, which combined all of the skills he had progressively learned. The result has been a forward transgression that naturally evolved to the point where he is now riding a bicycle at a stellar pace without any mishaps and very few falls, if any.

My journey to riding a bicycle was much different. When I was five, I participated in my father's "crash course" on riding a bicycle (heavy emphasis on "crash"). It wasn't until a few days into the ordeal, with skinned knees and elbows, that I was able to ride reasonably well, even though I continued to have small incidents and accidents until I had experienced several months of riding my bicycle. Moreover, the long-term effects of this crash course remain in the form of a few minor scars.

You might believe that the latter approach to riding a bicycle is the best. Just *get it done.* But I can tell you from experience that my oldest son has become a much more competent rider than I was, with better balance than I ever had. There are no scars (as of this writing!) and because we had a plan we started much earlier, which meant that he was actually more progressive and educated in balancing and pedaling (the two fundamentals of riding) by the same age that I first hopped on a bicycle. With these skills, my son was also able to quickly learn how to ride a small, motorized minibike that we purchased for him at the age of five, as well as have fun riding a scooter with kids much older than he is.

By taking a progressive approach to learning, acting as conductors and facilitating the process but progressively introducing and supporting him in applying tools that evolved his learning, we created a direction. Our multifaceted approach meant that his progress evolved much faster than had we applied the same rapid learning that I fell privy to.

In essence, we sped up by slowing down.

I'm not here to tell you to slow down, at least not specifically. What I do want to suggest is that by taking a methodical and patient approach to building team alignment in direction, you prepare the groundwork that allows for a steady increase in velocity. Notice I didn't say *speed*. Velocity is speed with an intended direction. If you speed, you get fined! Velocity is strategic speed—it is targeting a defined location, and then progressively applying speed in order to reach the intended target. Velocity has vision and purpose, whereas speed is blind.

By aligning the direction of the team, we create the groundwork for increasing velocity. Without the right groundwork in place (effective procedures, fluid processes, cross-functional collaboration, etc.) there is no clear vision, and hence any attempt to achieve more rapid results is simply blind speed.

More Is Not Less: Why Velocity Trumps Accuracy

Robert Browning once said, "Less is more,"[1] but the reality is that when it comes to empowering operations, this is simply not a possibility. Put another way, are your customers, board, or shareholders willing to wait patiently for new products, services, and levels of efficiency to be achieved? The answer is a clear no. When it comes to building a high-powered operation through empowered employees, speed actually trumps accuracy.

When it comes to NASCAR racing, the winners are not the individuals who took their time carefully driving around the track preserving their car, tires, and fuel; they're the individuals who put everything they had into winning the race, capitalizing on every opportunity to move ahead of their competitors. The same applies to hurdling; the racers who win are those who sprint the fastest when clearing the hurdles, not the individuals who take their time to jump over every hurdle. Even in the sport of golf, where precision and patience can mean the difference between par and birdie, those who hit the ball with the fastest swing tend to gain more distance, and a lower score.

In business, this same theory applies. Microsoft platforms are notorious for requiring updates and bug fixes after they are launched. The reason? Microsoft realizes that it is better to get a "good" product into the hands of its users, rather than hold back and wait to launch the "perfect" product. Automotive manufacturers such as Toyota and Ford are now historically releasing more frequent refreshes to their models in an effort to stay ahead of the competition. The idea of being that first to market and then making minor improvements along the way is now the preferred means to launch new products. The faster you can bring new models or products to market, the greater the opportunity you have of capturing market share.

Velocity surpasses accuracy any day.

Consider today what happens when an employee has a suggestion for an improvement in how something is done. In most businesses, be it service related or product related, the employee would share an idea with another employee to gain feedback and support. Once there is sufficient support for the idea, it would be raised to the supervisor, who in turn would consider the idea relative to the value it will provide based on the employees' feedback and how it will support the supervisor's objectives. The supervisor would then spend time considering the idea, and might in turn raise it to others for feedback (peers, other employees), before deciding whether to enact the change or seek further approval from management (for more information on this phenomenon, see my discussions on unqualified information in Chapter 1). This is a cumbersome and slow process, with each new step applying its own level of "validation" of the value the idea will provide. Why not simply allow the employee to take action on the idea?

Early in my career I worked for a large Fortune 500 company with several thousand employees. The high degree of regulation that impacted the industry, coupled with the sheer volume of employees, meant that moving an idea forward was a painfully slow process for anyone in the company. The result was low morale and lack of both motivation and innovation. This might sound harsh, but the greater the obstacles and validation steps between an employee idea and implementation of the idea, the greater the reduction in morale and in turn the less innovation that exists. In fact, innovation is based solely on velocity. There is more on this in Chapter 11.

It's important to mention at this point that by suggesting velocity surpasses accuracy, I'm not suggesting that we avoid planning or investing time in collaborating on solutions, or give short thrift to risk management planning. What I am suggesting is that the fewer the barriers (and in turn time) that exist between employee ideas and implementation of those ideas, the faster results will be attained, and when it comes to operational performance, it is the results that count!

I recently did some work with a large association where I brought together the employees as a group to discuss new ideas and ways to engage membership. During our discussions I asked the employees how they enjoyed spending time waiting for a response from a vendor or a colleague on a question they needed to know. The answer was overwhelmingly that they did not; after all, time is of the essence when it comes to getting things done. If this was the case then, I asked, would you guess that members, alliance partners, sponsors, and prospective members all value their time just as much, and thus would value a rapid and personalized response to their needs and inquiries? After brief consideration, once again the answer was yes. In fact, when I've compared the response times to members and customers across several associations and industries, it's apparent that there was a direct correlation between response time to members and the perceived value the association has to offer. It's better to get back to people right away, even if you don't have a specific response to their question, even if only to acknowledge receipt of the message and ensure that the stakeholders are aware of the priority their message carries, then to delay response until the best answer is found. This is a differentiator in the not-for-profit world, one in which velocity trumps accuracy.

There are three considerations to take into account when it comes to forming an environment that has diminished barriers between employee ideas and their integration:

1. **A community of sharing.** As we discussed in earlier chapters, a community is the optimum means of building a common vision and supportive momentum. That said, a community also accepts and nurtures feedback, ideas, and sharing. In order to ensure that ideas are shared openly and freely, executives and leadership across the company must nurture an environment where ideas are continually requested and valued. There must be a community of sharing.

2. **Comfort with ambiguity.** I recall from my school days that math was always a more challenging subject for me than English. The reason is not as you might expect. In math, grades are based solely on getting *the right answer.* Everything is black and white—there is little gray. One plus one equals two, no matter how you slice it. In English there is a significant amount of gray area, as higher grades are given to those who can dive deeply into literary mechanisms to ascertain deeper and greater meaning. Executives and leaders must be willing to reflect upon employee ideas, not against their preconceived notions of what is right and what is wrong, but of what value they might bring to the employees, the business, the customers, or the stakeholders. Leaders have to move away from everything being black and white and become comfortable with nurturing gray.

3. **Action oriented.** It's one thing to nurture an environment where ideas are free-flowing, but if the ideas can't be captured in a productive means, then they will offer little value. Of course you can invest in costly software to support this process such as iPlace by PricewaterhouseCoopers, but the reality is that a bank of ideas is only as good as its ability to be implemented. I'm a fan of the KISS approach (keep it short and simple), wherein ideas are captured daily by supervisors and managers at their team meetings, prompting immediate action on ideas that may offer low-risk, low-cost, and rapid results, all while logging more complex ideas to be

shared with cross-functional teams who will further investigate their implementation. . . . Note that the cross-functional teams I am referring to are not leadership-based, but employee-based with senior leader sponsorship.

Velocity, the ability to rapidly identify and act upon employee ideas in targeted areas empowering the operation in the process, is a much more powerful approach than spending time assessing and analyzing the value in employee ideas. In essence, the faster an idea can be captured, validated, and acted upon, the more quickly an improvement in performance (and results) can be achieved. Behavior that is reinforced becomes behavior that is adopted, and through this cycle a vortex of action is created. As employees recognize and become comfortable with making and acting upon recommendations, their desire and willingness to do so increases.

Referring to my example of a hurdler earlier in this chapter, who do you think has a better chance at winning the race, the hurdler who immediately launches into the race the very moment the gun goes off, or the methodical racer who takes a slower approach, trying not to hit any hurdles, run into other lanes, or lose pace? My bet is on the former.

Progressive Velocity: The Operational Improvement Vortex

In early 2015, I took a survey of two dozen employees across five different manufacturing, distribution, and service-related industries asking one very simple question: What is the single greatest obstacle to improving performance in your company?

The answers were as follows in order of priority:

1. The speed at which management takes action on making improvements.
2. The inability of management to listen and act upon employee concerns.
3. The lack of planning and inconsistency in management change initiatives.

4. Ineffective technology, tools, or equipment to effectively do the job.
5. Insufficient time and resources to complete work as required by management.

If we contrast these responses against the top five strategies that CEOs perceive as necessary to improve operational performance,[2] we can see conflicting views:

1. Raise employee engagement and productivity.
2. Focus on reduction of baseline costs.
3. Break down internal silos.
4. Continual improvement.
5. Better alignment between strategy, objectives, and the organization.

Whose views do you think are most accurate? Better yet, whose views do you think are more important? When you notice the differences between these viewpoints relative to *how* operational performance can be improved, it identifies several very distinct gaps:

- We've been beating the drum in these areas for decades, yet we've experienced very little recognizable improvement in morale, productivity, or performance.
- All of the CEO strategies (employee engagement, cost reduction, collaboration, continuous improvement) are areas that can be tied to "programs," which puts them at risk of becoming "just another management initiative."
- These are for the most part intangible, failing to get at the root of why we fail to improve operational performance.
- These are most likely strategies that were identified to the CEOs by their direct reports, not coming from employees.
- There is nothing "quick" about achieving any of these initiatives.

In essence, we continue to beat the drums of engagement and continuous improvement, which hinge solely on our ability to interact with and empower employees, yet the very idea of employee empowerment is not on most CEO's radar. The greater our focus on building a community of empowered employees, one in which managers prompt, support, and facilitate employee ideas rather than vet and validate ideas to serve their own objectives, the more quickly we will improve operational performance.

Several years ago I created the Operational Improvement Vortex (Figure 6.2) as a means of identifying precisely how the velocity at which operational improvement occurs in this type of environment steadily increases as the response to and integration of employee ideas occur.

FIGURE 6.2 Operational Improvement Vortex

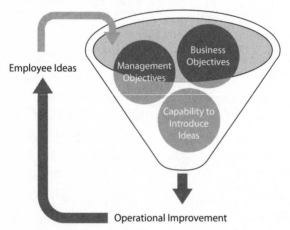

In the matrix, you will notice that a reduction in the circumference of any of the three elements will provide space for the remaining elements to increase in size (and velocity). In essence:

1. A decrease in the focus on business and management objectives provides more room for flow through employee ideas.
2. The faster the ideas are introduced into the operation, the faster the ideas will flow from employees to improvement.
3. The faster that employees witness improvements to the operation, the faster and more valuable the ideas they introduce will become.

In both instances, employees are the critical component to success. *The value of ideas identified* is based on the value to employees. If there is little perceived value to employees in introducing and incorporating new ideas to improve operational performance, then there is little commitment to supporting the idea. *If there is in turn little commitment* on behalf of the employees to pursuing or supporting improvement ideas, there is little chance the ideas or initiatives will survive.

A few years ago I sat on the board of directors for an organization, during which we spent several days in a retreat formulating the business strategy. Despite the preparation time, discussion around challenges and opportunities, and even the tangible value of ideas generated, several years later the strategy was failing to deliver the intended results. Did we have the strategic objectives wrong? Was our vision weak or incorrect? The answer in both instances was no. Our issue was in how the strategy was introduced to employees.

A strategy is a form of continuous improvement—it is, if created correctly, a plan to improve the organization's performance in pursuit of the vision. The board I was part of had a CEO who was not a strong leader, nor was he engaging with employees. In fact, he interacted with employees very little, choosing instead to rely on his senior executives for advice and guidance—and to roll out the board's strategy. The result was a lack of adoption of the objectives by employees, a lack of progress toward the objectives, and an inability to effect change at the association's operational level. The strategy failed on account of the CEO's inability to help his leadership team and employees connect with the value of the strategy and objectives, and thereby an inability to create commitment to achieving the objectives.

After 24 months of failed progress (amid other challenges with the CEO), we were forced to let him go. Today, with a new and highly engaging CEO at the helm and some changes to senior executive staff and the board, there is a significant shift in the morale of the staff as well as a progressive improvement in operational performance. Surveying the employees, it became clear that they perceived value in making improvements and thereby were committed to taking consistent action to effect the changes necessary.

If there's something you take away from this chapter, I hope it's that speed kills. In business, being first to market is important, but being first to market with a product or service that's of poor quality, little value, or is easily repeatable or replaceable by competitors will result in lost opportunities, lost customers, and a loss in market position. Attention needs to shift from "speed" to "velocity":

1. Be specific about what you should focus your energy, resources, and investment on—introduce and pursue improvements in processes, resources, products, and services that provide unique and distinct advantage in the marketplace.
2. Balance time and resources invested with the priority of desired results. Not everything is or should be a priority. Identify changes or improvements that will yield the greatest value (to customers, the business, employees, the market) and plan accordingly.
3. Oversee the orchestra that creates your music. Achieving the optimal speed to introduce improvements requires someone with oversight *and* foresight. Choose your conductor carefully.
4. Be specific about where you intend to be and when. The goal is not to blindly introduce improvements, but to ensure you meet milestones that will validate you are on the right track, and allowing enough time to make adjustments and ensure your changes or improvements are as valuable as possible.
5. Don't overthink. It's one thing to have a plan that you follow; it's another to get stuck in the weeds, overthinking what "the next step" should be. Although speed kills, it doesn't kill nearly as quickly as standing still. Focus on velocity over accuracy.

Through increased velocity we can achieve more powerful results that benefit the business, its employees, and its stakeholders. But what of the customers? After all, without customers a business will cease to survive or exist. In the next chapter we will discuss the customer value connection, how to build a stronger connection between your employees and customers to support greater value in the outcomes of your operational objectives and improvements.

PART 3

Collaborative Power

Throughout the previous chapters we've been discussing how to initiate interactions at different levels across the organization to improve communication and broaden perspective. It's simply not enough however, to expect that initiating such interactions with others, in and of itself, will improve the performance of business operations. There must in turn be a mechanism by which this level of interaction can be harnessed and converted to viable outcomes. This is where the application of intentionally strategic collaboration, with internal and external sources of the organization, nurtured and harvested in the correct manner, can actually have a significant and positive impact on operational effectiveness.

In Part 3, we will discuss the various sources of collaboration and how specifically to introduce and incorporate various levels of collaboration in order to improve productivity, gain efficiencies, reduce costs, and create perpetual and profitable customer value.

In the following chapters, we will introduce the concept of productive collaboration, the outcome of powerful and purposeful interactions with collaborative sources that will elevate your operational performance well beyond the level that any individually focused program or initiative could.

7

The Value Connection

What Your Customers and Employees Really Want

What we value as customers has and will continue to evolve. As we discussed earlier, our investment habits are becoming more closely tied to personalization and convenience rather than price and quality. The habits that are influencing our spending behaviors are in turn impacting how we as individuals behave in our jobs and our corporate environments. The convenience of buying online, as an example, has influenced how companies offer products to their customers. Westway Electric Supply began selling its products online in 2001 and has since refined its processes to make the selection, purchase, and delivery of products as streamlined as possible. Why would the company do this? Two reasons. First, its customers have less time to travel to their location to browse inventory, instead identifying and purchasing goods during after-hours from the comfort of their home or office. Second, online giants such as Amazon could consume the business if it doesn't offer similar services and convenience in order to compete. I tell every manufacturer or distributor that I meet: if you can put a part number on it, then Amazon can sell it, and it can likely do it cheaper and faster than you ever could.

The tables have turned, and customers rather than companies are now in charge of the entire buying process. For example, banks now offer numerous ways to manage your money aside from visiting the actual bank, all for the sake of convenience and catering to their customers' preferences, whatever they might be. With this said, let's take a moment to consider why companies are increasingly catering to the needs of their customers. Here are just a few reasons:

1. Increasing competition globally for customer attention and cash.
2. The ability of customers to respond in real time using platforms like social media to say whatever they want about a company, product, or service.
3. The increasing sensitivity of company brands to more educated and demanding customers.

In 2008, United Airlines damaged musician Dave Carroll's $3,500 Taylor guitar during a stopover at O'Hare airport in Chicago, Illinois.[1] Despite his attempts to receive assistance from several United Airlines employees, Carroll was unable to resolve the situation. He then filed a claim with United for the damage, but again was denied assistance when his claim was deemed to have missed the 24-hour deadline for submission following damage. In frustration, Dave Carroll produced a music video documenting the experience and posted it on YouTube. The result was a staggering 150,000 views in the video's first day. Today, nearly eight years later, the video is still live on YouTube and has had over 14 million views. Has this impacted the perceptions of United's business since its inception? Absolutely. Has the impact likely exceeded the cost of replacing the $3,500 guitar? Absolutely.

In this instance it took executives at United to step in and bring resolution to the problem, but only after the video garnered considerable attention on YouTube. Worse yet, their actions to resolve Carroll's problem ventured outside the normal United protocol. Had employees been more empowered to operate outside of existing protocols and processes, the issue would likely have been resolved at its origin, before Carroll ever produced the video that caused such a PR nightmare. In an age when customers are in greater control of the buying experience, the connection between customers and employees is absolutely 100 percent crucial. Put another way, failing to empower employees to immediately satisfy customer needs (such as the case of Dave Carroll above) can be detrimental, if not fatal, for any business, in any sector, of any size. The reality is, however, that with the existence of the communication disconnect that we discussed in earlier chapters, it's simply unrealistic to believe that executives can remain in tune with every customer interaction, interjecting when necessary to ensure a positive customer experience. It's also unrealistic to expect that a process or technology can be formulated to provide the directions and empowerment necessary to allow an employee the ability to ensure that every customer interaction is a positive experience. Empowering employees in how a business operates is the only means to ensure that every customer experience is a positive one. We must create a connection between the value customers seek and the value employees are empowered to provide. This is what I call the value connection.

In this chapter we will discuss the factors that influence the value connection, as well as how to build a business that can meet the needs and demands of today's customers.

What Your Customers Value and Why It's Important

Value is a funny thing. When it comes to operating a business, the ability to attract and retain customers results from the ability to offer the perception of value. The challenge is that what customers value evolves and is often very unpredictable. RIM, producer of the BlackBerry, knew that its competition was moving toward providing touch-screen technology, but the company believed that customers placed considerable value in the QWERTY keyboard, hence it decided to continue to offer a keyboard at a time when virtually all of its competition, including Apple and Samsung, was moving to a touch screen. The result was the rapid decline in demand for the BlackBerry. RIM's perception of what its customers would value in the future was based on its success from the past. Not surprisingly they were wrong, and the loss of market share and profitability is the evidence to prove such.

Each and every year, I work with a few business associations that struggle with how to attract and retain their members. The struggle, which is really more of a misperception, is that members want the same things they did from associations 5 or even 10 years ago. They don't. I sat on the board of a not-for-profit association for several years. At virtually every meeting, we would discuss the lack of interest among members to attend networking events, although their desire for knowledge and interaction remained quite high. Aside from these conversations, several employees collaborated on compiling information from members and experts alike, building an online forum where members could access research and knowledge. The knowledge portal, as it was coined, was more of a whim developed by employees in response to membership needs than it was a strategic offer of value to members, but it gained significant attention and traction with members almost immediately. So much so that other similar associations began to request access to the knowledge portal for their members. Members desired access to the information; however, what they valued was no longer the personal interaction, but instead the ability to access the information instantly and at a convenient time for them. What the members valued had shifted.

We can look at our own personal lives and see how what we value evolves, both individually and as a collective society. I recall that when I was 16, in order to access your own money, it was considered the norm to only visit the bank between the hours of 9:00 a.m. and 12:00 p.m. or 1:00 p.m. and 4:00 p.m., Monday through Friday. You either attended during these hours to deal with the teller, or you went without money, simple as that. Moreover, if you couldn't make it, you also couldn't send someone in your place. The advent of automatic teller machines influenced what we as consumers expected from banks, as has the Internet. Why, for example, would I visit a bank during their banking hours to access my money if I could collect money from a bank machine that resided at any 7-Eleven? To compete, banks were forced to introduce longer hours and more convenience options. This evolution continues today as banks are moving from requiring customers to show up to review and sign mortgage payments and open new accounts to offering in-house visits and more convenient online offerings. This shift in how banks service customers is a result of the evolution of their business in order to provide continued value to their customers. I predict that in 15 years, the brick-and-mortar bank will no longer exist.

If we consider how our customers' perceptions of value have evolved, there has been a distinct shift from servicing *us* (meeting the general needs and collective values of large groups of people) to servicing *me* (meeting the needs of individuals, providing more options and conveniences, and handing over control to the customer).

The way in which this plays out in business is both simple and complex. In order to meet the perceived value of customers today, it's critical to focus on serving individuals. That often means more options. Allowing a customer the opportunity to call, e-mail, or chat to someone live in order to answer a product or service question is quite common, but what's become more prevalent is the need to provide e-mail response on the same day and provide live chat and telephone service 24 hours a day, 7 days a week. Customers want instantaneous response and support, which means greater cost. Moreover, the practice of subcontracting this service out to a country that may not speak your customer's language as its first language is also passé. During a recent call to my local phone company, I was placed on hold briefly; the message began with "proudly serving you from Canada."

You may be thinking by this point that attempting to learn and understand what it is that your customers desire will be too costly or too difficult. Fortunately, you're wrong. In fact, to stay in synch with your customer needs as they evolve can be as simple as asking them. I frequently book flights using Flightnetwork.com, a very convenient service that is intuitive to use and cost-effective. I was pleased with the service for some time; however, as a result of needing to change a flight reservation, I actually had to call the company. My impressions quickly changed. After being on hold for more than 15 minutes (and listening to that famed prerecorded message "Our call volumes are higher than expected; please be stand by for the next agent"), it took several more minutes to resolve what in the end was a very simple problem. More than a month later I had to call again, and once again I was faced with the same wait times. It's clear that their high call volumes were actually their normal call volumes, and should be expected. From my experience, Flightnetwork.com, unfortunately, had failed to make changes to diminish these volumes. Although I still use Flightnetwork.com for travel today, I have introduced other travel partners that I use for trips with more stopovers, as I have no intent of being placed on hold for such a long period of time again. Despite the competitive price and convenience of Flightnetwork.com, a poor call response time has cost the company a percentage of my business, and quite likely other customers as well. The solution, of course, would be to hire more phone attendants and/or streamline processes related to call response times, but it's likely that this service would equate to additional cost and overhead. Would Flightnetwork.com gain a return on its investment if it did so? My guess is that, that is the question the company is most likely still pondering today as its customer base slowly erodes.

This brings me to my second point about customer value. Great marketing can mask a company's inability to provide value to its customers. Put another way, I might have an attractive or appealing service that great marketing will ensure attracts new customers, but if the service doesn't deliver the value my prospective customers expect it to (the marketing outsold the value of the product or service), then my ability to retain customers is weak. If the rate by which customers depart is less than the rate by which I attract new customers (as a result of great marketing), then I may not see clearly how the actual value of my product or service does not satisfy my customers' perception of its value.

Recall the association I referred to earlier that had significant success with the creation of its member knowledge portal. This was a significant win for the association, as it had been struggling with how to retain membership once educational needs had been met (through its certification programs). Members no longer valued attending network events, nor did they seem to have interest in volunteering and getting involved with the association. The marketing of the certification program and the credentials it contained attracted a significant cross-section of potential members, but what it did not do was address what members valued once the certification had been achieved. Great marketing to attract members was not helping to retain them once the credentials were obtained. The way to retain members once they signed up was to first provide value that met with expectations, followed by continuous value that served the ongoing needs of the association's new and existing members.

The third consideration relative to customer value is how employees can make or break a customer's value experience. You can design and offer a highly valuable product or service, but if employees do not build or deliver value in the intended manner, then the customer will not receive value as you or they expect.

Earlier this year I transitioned my television, telephone, and Internet service from several individual providers to Rogers. I made this change based on the perception of value that was stacked in Rogers' favor, specifically:

- Competitive pricing achieved as a result of bundling all of our services
- Less disruption with television signals by shifting from satellite to cable
- Faster Internet speeds
- The ability to record television shows on a personal video recorder (PVR)

When the gentlemen came to install and connect the various services (the first point-of-contact for receiving the value I had expected), my perception of value in Rogers's service quickly diminished. The installation was sloppy, with wire scraps being strewn about the house; not all of the televisions were connected on account of a missing adapter that the installer could not locate in his truck; Internet service was completely disabled for hours due to the installer's inability to take the steps necessary to create my Internet account (which he suggested was the responsibility of customer service); and lastly customer service was unable to connect my Internet service on account of the installers not logging job order completion notes. Although the initial perceived value of the switch in providers did exist, the changeover to Rogers was horrendous, and as such it diminished any perceptions I had of value in making the change.

My dislike for Rogers came about quickly, but interestingly it was extinguished less than 24 hours later when I received a call from Rogers customer care who asked about my experience. After explaining the catastrophe that had occurred, the individual in customer care (who was clearly empowered to resolve such situations) took steps to resolve all of the issues, also offering 60 days of no charge on-demand movies as a consolation. Although it's possible that she was going to offer me the movies regardless of my dissatisfaction with the installation, her demeanor and candor eased the pain of the less-than-valuable experience, and to date (nearly six months later) all of the value I expected by moving my business to Rogers has been realized. My perceptions of value were quickly diminished by a single employee, and then slowly improved by the actions of a different employee.

An employee can make or break a customer's value experience. This in turn means that employees must:

1. Be clear on what customers value in the products or services a business offers.
2. Be empowered to take action when and if a customer is not satisfied with the value received.
3. Have the resources, knowledge, and skills available to ensure value is delivered to customers.
4. Believe in the value that the product or service offers and be able to explain and engage their customers in that value.
5. Be enthusiastic and passionate about the company and its products and/or services and be able to extend that passion to their customers.

Customer value is, as I alluded to earlier, a perception. That perception is either met, not met, or exceeded by employees. Therefore providing customer value requires that employees are clear on, connect with, and empowered to deliver value to customers. Without these three fundamental components, customers will fail to be satisfied, and employees will lack the motivation to deliver.

Customer Collaboration: Building an Operation with a Foundation in Value

If business success results from creating a strong customer-employee connection in order to deliver consistently high levels of value to the customer, then how can we be sure what is the right value, the right time, and the right forum for delivery? The answer is through customer collaboration.

In today's day and age, customers have their finger on the trigger aimed directly at your brand, and they can shoot at any time. A less-than-valuable experience can result in negative or even defamatory comments hitting the Internet in mere minutes, ruining decades of hard work and investment. You've likely seen the video of a FedEx employee throwing a parcel at the front door of a customer during delivery, or heard about the server who was fired for posting a receipt from a disgruntled customer who chose not to leave a tip. You've heard of these incidents because in today's world, the customer is in control. This may seem counterintuitive, but despite significant investments in marketing and development of the most robust and unique products or services, a company's reputation (and its revenue) can be diminished in minutes by a dissatisfied customer who possesses the energy, resources, and social media intelligence to take action.

Tony Hseih, cofounder and CEO of Zappos, was aware of the power of today's customer when he partnered with Nick Swinmurn to create the online shoe retailer. From the beginning, Tony and Nick were clear about three basic rules that would govern the company:

1. Zappos was a service company first that happened to sell shoes.
2. It would rather invest money on improving the customer experience than marketing.
3. It would have to retrain its employees from wanting to minimize their time spent interacting with customers.

With the customers in control of their own experience by collaborating with employees, Zappos grew like wildfire, reaching $252 million in sales in less than six years under Hseih's control.

Zappos' story is unique in that it was selling a commodity (shoes) in an unorthodox manner—sight unseen except via the Internet—with operating costs that were higher than similar competitors by operating a 24x7 high-cost warehouse operation and choosing to ship all customer orders from the Zappos warehouse rather than drop ship from manufacturers. Its success is built upon the ability to collaborate with its customers to provide products and an experience that is consistently valuable, despite the shifting perspectives on what value might be perceived as.

Collaborating with customers requires a shift away from the traditional notions of sales and customer service. A customer is no longer a "target" or "market" but a partner that can support the formulation and growth of a powerful business that stands out from competitors. There are several considerations that must be in place for customer collaboration to exist:[2]

1. **Customers must be heard.** Do you remember the commercial from the eighties in which a little old lady bellowed, "Where's the beef?" The commercial was Wendy's attempt to draw consumers to the fact that its rivals McDonalds and Burger King had larger buns then Wendy's, thereby making the burger falsely appear larger. In sequels to the commercial, Clara Peller, the actor who played the role of the little old lady, was seen calling executives from the large bun competitors asking them over the telephone, "Where's the beef?"[3] The commercial and its sequels pointed out a very prominent fact. Customers must be provided a convenient forum to vent their concerns, and where there is no forum, they will find their own. Consider, for example, that there are over 304 million monthly active users on Twitter, all of whom can send out a tweet in a matter of seconds without further consideration as to how their frustrations may appear or be interpreted, good or bad.

2. **Customer intelligence is gold.** Customer feedback that fails to be captured and used to improve business performance is a lost opportunity to provide value. During a recent trip with my family, we used the drive-in window at a Dunkin' Donuts to buy some

assorted Munchkins. We received our order, and as we drove away I happened to look into the box to find virtually all of the Munchkins were the same flavor. Irritated, I turned the car around and drove back through to ask for the problem to be resolved. The employee apologized and suggested that at the time I drove through (only five minutes earlier) there had been only one flavor of Munchkin available. In return, I asked whether this was something the employee thought she might instead share with the customer in the future rather than assuming it was acceptable. Fortunately she agreed. Do you think this example made it back to someone who could in turn review and reinforce the value of ensuring customer orders are filled right the first time and every time with all employees? Likely not. This is feedback that will likely go unheard and will lead to similar occurrences happening again and again, slowly eroding customer trust, and the perceived value of the brand, and of the location.

3. **Customer needs take precedence.** As a frequent traveler, I will admit that I periodically stop at McDonald's. I've found that most of the franchises I've visited have made a considerable effort to ensure greeting customers and taking their order quickly upon arrival; however, following the collection of money, the process seems to erode. Recently while visiting a McDonald's in Toronto, I was quickly greeted and served by a smiling and enthusiastic employee. However, once I provided payment, my receipt was placed on the counter, and the attendant turned her attention to the next customer. I looked around for what to do next (where should I stand, how will I track my receipt, do I have time to grab a straw from the shelf behind me?) and noticed that all of the customers were doing the same thing. No one knew where to stand or what to do next. The employees who were consolidating orders, watching screens, and hitting buttons (apparently to stop the constant beeping) were clearly confused as well, as they weren't fulfilling orders in the same order they were being taken and were running up and down the counter yelling out various products that they were still short like "Big Mac," or "apple pie."

The chaos made it clear as to why McDonald's takes money up front. All employees regardless of their role or department must understand that the customer takes priority, and it's through providing a seamless and customer-centric experience that priority is demonstrated and satisfied.

4. **Employees must be empowered to provide value.** I've been using Sirius XM in my car for several years. The value to someone such as myself, a frequent traveler who spends hours in a car each week, is worth the investment. Following the purchase of my last car, I called Sirius to extend my membership as the trial period was about to expire. I had also decided to add this service to my wife's car, so I expected I would receive something that was less than the published price. After a few minutes speaking to the customer service agent, it was clear that either Sirius no longer offered any promotions for signing on a new account (which was not what its website suggested), or the employee with whom I was speaking did not have the ability to help with my request. I asked to speak to a manager, and 15 minutes later not only had I extended my service at no cost, but I had signed on my wife's account at a less than published price and would enjoy the benefits of My SXM for the next 12 months at no additional charge. The question this presents, however, is why did I have to escalate my issue to the manager in order to achieve the outcomes and value I desired? Contrast this experience with companies like the Marriot who actually provide their employees with a budget of over $2,000 in order to ensure that each and every customer's stay is relaxing and enjoyable. Like the Marriot, employees must be empowered to provide value if the experience is going to be seamless and stress-free for customers.

The Employee-Customer Connection (ECC)

My friend Gary has been a director of customer service for a global technology company for over a decade. He and his team manage hundreds of inbound customer inquiries and complaints on a daily basis, and despite the complexity of requests that flow into the call center, there are only a few key points that he and his team are measured on:

1. How quickly his team responds to inbound customer calls.
2. How quickly the customer concern is addressed and the call is closed.
3. How satisfied customers are with the speed and accuracy of their experience with the call center.

When you look at these guidelines, ask yourself a question: Are these the metrics that best serve the needs of the customer or the company? I think you will find they serve the interests of the latter more than the former. For call centers, as an example, this is the standard business model in which time equates to money. The faster customer inquiries and concerns can be addressed and closed, the better the performance appears to be for the call center, and often the greater the compensation that is provided to the center (for offering the service) and the employees (for their performance). There is rarely any consideration for the level of *value* the customer obtained from the call. This is a counterintuitive model to what companies like Zappos, which I discussed earlier in this chapter, use in how they interact with customers. Tony Hseih has been quoted[4] as saying that he and his business partner realized early on that when they opened a call center in Las Vegas they would have to retrain many of their new hires from how they had been taught to interact with customers. This was due to the large numbers of individuals employed in the industry. Tony realized that virtually any company could sell shoes online, but in order to build a profitable and longstanding company, he had to ensure that Zappos' employees made a connection with each and every customer they interacted with. Every customer-employee interaction must create value for the customer.

To achieve this, Tony ensured that several key considerations were incorporated into the business model:[5]

1. **Time available.** For an employee to truly build a connection with customers and best serve their interests, time must be available.

Employees' performance should not be measured by how quickly they serve customers, but in how satisfied the customers feel following the interaction.

2. **Knowledge of the product line.** Putting customers on hold to ask questions is annoying, so employees must be completely versed in the products that the company offers so they can quickly and effectively match customer desires with company offerings.

3. **Knowledge of the market.** Tony realized that not every customer would find value in the products that Zappos offered, so employees had to be aware of what else was in the market and what competitors were offering in order to ascertain early on when Zappos might not be able to best serve customer needs.

4. **Put customer needs first.** Where employees assessed that customers would be best served by the products or services of competitors, they were encouraged to not only redirect the customer to competitors, but help them to get there, providing necessary contact information and following up at a later date to ensure that the customer had found what he or she was looking for.

5. **Empowered.** There are stories from Zappos of employees investing company money to send free replacements for shoes and other accessories and gifts to customers when the employee deemed it would increase the value of the interaction. This investment rarely required the permission of management and was employee behavior that was both encouraged and supported.

Historically it has been the job of sales and marketing to interact with the customer, manage the relationship, and provide feedback to those within the business as to what the customer wants. Relative to the needs and desires of today's customer, there is one significant problem with this approach. People in sales are, in most instances, paid to sell, not to spend considerable amounts of their time hanging out with customers to learn more about what they value in the products and services (both those currently offered by the seller's company and those that aren't) that are offered today, and those that might be offered in the future. Furthermore, those in sales are often trained and incentivized to "make the sale," not obtain customer intelligence and in turn share it with the organization. There are, of course, exceptions to this rule, as there are with most rules. I have met salespeople who do recognize that time invested with customers is time well spent, not only for them but for the future of their company; however, this is not the norm.

Let me take a moment here to provide you with a more specific example of delivering customer value through an empowered employee-customer connection.

Early in my corporate career while in the role of materials manager, I was forwarded a telephone call from the president of one of our customer companies. She had received delivery of our products, but the truck driver (a third-party carrier that we used for the shipment) had been belligerent and rude to both her personnel and herself. She had called our customer service team to complain, and the team members had quickly (presumably to pass along responsibility for the issue) forwarded the call to me to address. After discussing the president's concerns with her, I took immediate action with the following steps:

1. I called the carrier to notify the company that the driver used was never to move our goods again.
2. I confirmed that the nearly $250,000 in annual business the carrier held with us was now at risk, and I expected the company to provide the customer with a formal apology, as well as an action plan for me as to how they would ensure that this type of behavior never impacted our customers again.
3. I requested a written apology sent to my attention by the carrier immediately that outlined the interim actions the carrier was going to take within the next 24 hours.
4. I called the president to provide an update on status, and to tell her that I would be forwarding the e-mail upon receipt, and would call again before the end of the next business day.
5. I followed up as promised.

The president was overjoyed at my response, not because of what I had done as much as how quickly I had responded. She valued the speed with which I dealt with the situation. Fortunately, I was in a position where I was able to take action in the areas outlined above; however, I also reviewed this situation with my staff members in the event that they ever received a similar call. Had I or my team focused only on our objectives (ship goods on time and without damage), then this concern would have been less of a priority. Fortunately, the owner of our company at the time was a strong proponent of ensuring an employee-customer connection, investing significant time and resources in helping employees understand how they are empowered to provide value to the company's customers.

Through my ongoing work with companies in creating strong employee-customer connections, I have coined the term ECC as a means to identify how all employees have a responsibility as it pertains to supporting the customer, and how a closer connection between employees and customers supports a more powerful and sustainable company and operation (Figure 7.1).

FIGURE 7.1 Employee-Customer Connection

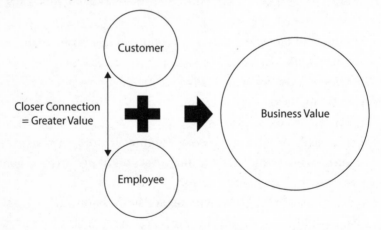

As a CEO or executive you must facilitate the employee-customer connection. In some recent work with a large automotive servicing chain, I found that customer-facing managers and employees whose role was to manage customer relationships (including quoting, fulfillment, addressing quality concerns) were spending the predominance of their day behind a computer looking up and requoting costs and structuring quotes in order to ensure customers received the "best price" the "first time." Yet when I interviewed customers, they perceived significantly less value in a company that spent significant effort attempting to obtain them "the best price" and instead preferred to obtain a more personalized and proactive relationship. Rather than provide quotes on identified needs, they wanted a business that partnered with them to identify needs before they became apparent, to offer on-site support in managing inventory, and to provide onsite resources to support project execution. In essence, for my client to offer their employees free coffee and a lounge was great, but if service attendants never had the opportunity to get out from behind their desk in order to meet and interact with customers, then the customer's experience was less valuable. Interestingly, the findings demonstrated that the current approach by my client was doing little more then making their service a commodity, rather than a value-added partner. In addition, employees were frustrated with not having the opportunity to get out and meet with their customers. Their model offered little value to the customer as a result of lacking an employee-customer connection.

It is only through creating a closer connection between employees and customers that we can add value to customers' businesses and lives, and it is through value that we increase retention of existing customers *and* at the same time attract new customers. In my experience, the days of selling are dead; it's only through building an employee-customer connection that companies can explore collaborative customer relationships, offering perpetual business growth opportunities that serve to steadily increase profitability.

The Evolution of Customer Value

In 1984, my father purchased a brand new Pontiac Parisienne Brougham. We had traveled the countryside looking at new cars for several months, and prior to purchasing the Pontiac my father had seriously considered a 1984 Chevrolet Caprice Classic. The two are virtually the exact same car, but the Caprice was, as they would say back in 1984, loaded. With power windows, power locks, and air conditioning, and I'm dating myself here, it truly was a car of the future. Although it was by all intents and purposes the exact same car as the Pontiac, my father's final decision was to purchase the Pontiac for three reasons:

1. The Pontiac had wire wheels and whitewalls, which my father preferred.
2. The Pontiac was at a dealership that was closer to our home, making it easier for warranty and service work.
3. All of those power options were just another reason for something to break.

We kept the Pontiac for nearly six years, at the end of which my father had a few concerns that he was going to make sure were addressed in his next car:

1. The wire wheels were a pain to clean, as were the whitewalls.
2. He had serviced the car at a local dealership (not the one he purchased from), so he was going to try to give that local dealership his future business.
3. He was tired of rolling up the window with a crank, which often broke due to the continuous pressure.

What a difference only six years made—and that was over two decades ago. What my father had valued when he first purchased the car had become the supporting reasons for why he was going to trade the car six years later. Our perceptions of value, like my father's, evolve over time, and as a result companies must remain at the forefront of understanding exactly what customers value if they are going to be able to offer products or services that are valued (and in turn support continued profitability) on a continuum.

It's clear then that as society evolves, in turn our perceptions of value evolve. In today's information age, when a vast array of information can be obtained at a speed faster than ever before, our perceptions are evolving more rapidly, as well as becoming increasingly diverse.

Now that I've got you thinking further about the evolution of value, let's consider how customer value is evolving, and some of the key areas in which customers are making greater demands than they have previously. Specifically we will discuss points that virtually any organization, be it product based, service based, or even a not-for-profit, is faced with in today's day and age.

> **Real-time response.** Customers today are valuing (in fact demanding) instantaneous response. Wait times to any degree are simply unacceptable on account of the ability to obtain information quickly. It used to be that it might take time to find the answer to a question through discussions with friends or coworkers, or even searching through the encyclopedia (gasp!). Today we can obtain answers to almost any question instantaneously by using services such as Google and Bing. The ability to obtain instantaneous answers have trained consumers to demand the same of companies. Our patience has grown short and continues to diminish; hence greater value is perceived from those organizations that can respond instantaneously, providing a personal response to meet our needs. A longtime client of mine in the steel manufacturing industry recently introduced live-chat technology to his website, managed by one of his highly capable and knowledgeable younger employees. In the first 90 days he saw 20 new leads converted to two final sales. This was an avenue that he and his sales manager had never previously considered until our conversations around customer value resulted in the conclusion that the company's customers were using its website more and more (as seen in traffic numbers) to research new products. By capitalizing on real-time responses, this relatively low-tech company has now leaped light-years ahead of their competition.
>
> **Customization.** In today's society we are inundated with options, and these options have created a demand for customization. Growing up, I worked in a grocery store stocking shelves. At that time the cereal aisle was one of the most congested aisles in the store relative to options. There were dozens of brands, sizes, and options

available to customers who desired cereal. Venture into a grocery store today, and you will find twice the options in choice of cereals, broken into categories such as gluten-free cereals, all-natural cereals, sugar-free cereals, children's cereals, and so on. This choice of options has created significant challenges for manufacturers, who were used to producing few products in high volumes and are now forced to shift how they manufacture in order to produce smaller lots of a greater number of SKUs. This complexity in turn has led to the need to increase employee skill and capabilities, reduce equipment change over times, and increase inventory storage, fulfillment speed, and accuracy. The list goes on. The demand for increased options and customization, which will only increase in the decades ahead, has in turn driven a spike through the heart of mass production.

Perceptions of time. The complexities outlined above are making it more and more difficult for manufacturing companies to meet customer needs in reasonable time periods. Lead times are, in many instances, growing rather than diminishing. Furthermore, the ability to purchase virtually anything from the comfort of our living room has shifted our perceptions about how long it should take to obtain a product or service. The digital revolution has in effect changed our perceptions of time, and not necessarily for the better. One of my clients that manufacturers custom wooden products prides itself on being able to produce custom one-off furniture that will meet the dreams and desires of its customers. The only challenge is, however, that as its customers demand greater customization, their willingness to accept a reasonable lead time to deliver their customized product is diminishing. Where a lead time of three to four weeks (to source and obtain lumber, manufacture, stain, outfit with fixtures, and deliver) was considered reasonable only a few short years ago, customers today want greater customization in one to two weeks. It's possible that internal lead times to produce these products can be reduced somewhat, but my client is at the mercy of the lumber producer, a much larger company that is unwilling to ship specialized wood in a reduced time period.

Increased availability. Considering the influences of customization and a changing perception of the time it should take to obtain products and services, you might think that we expect that not all of the plethora of options for any one product or service might be available (as we generally understand the challenges in providing everything to everyone), but in fact it's quite the opposite. The idea that a product or service may not be readily available is increasingly becoming unacceptable to the general public. A couple of years ago I visited my local cell phone retailer to purchase a new iPhone 5. I was clear going into the store that I didn't want a 5C or a 5S; I wanted a 5. The retail clerk was quite supportive of my decision, but after 10 minutes of searching the back room she came to the conclusion that the store didn't have an iPhone 5 in stock. I stood almost in shock for a moment at the thought that I might actually have to return at a later date, and seeing my dismay she quickly suggested I visit a retailer a few stores down that might actually have the phone. If it did, I could purchase the phone from that store and then return to her for activation. Fortunately (and almost to my surprise), the idea worked, and even today I'm thankful for the creative and supportive efforts of this one employee. Interestingly, however, unlike Zappos she made it clear that I wasn't to tell "her boss," as she would likely get in trouble for sending me elsewhere to purchase the phone. As consumers and customers, we are demanding increased availability and are more than willing to move our business elsewhere if our demands aren't met.

Brand influence. I would be remiss if I didn't take a moment to discuss the influence that social media has had and will continue to have on the perceptions of customer value. From the story I mentioned earlier of Dave Carroll who took to social media to present his case against United Airlines following significant damage to his custom guitar, to more recent examples such as McDonald's failed attempt at using the hashtag #McDStories to present positive stories of the quality and origin of its food, social media has offered an outlet for consumers and customers to voice their discontent with a product or service. No time barriers, no filters, and no conscience. Simply put, companies that avoid managing their presence and interactions with customers on social media are leaving themselves open to the risk of damaging their brand. A single discontented customer can ruin something that has taken a decade to build, in only a few minutes. Social media has supported (and influenced) our need for real-time response; hence the continued growth and adoption of social media will further support and influence our needs in the near future.

Regardless of your company or industry, whether you are a for-profit or not-for-profit organization, the above influences on customer value perceptions will continue to evolve over time. In virtually every instance the means by which to navigate, manage, and capitalize on these influences is through employees.

- More creative and empowered employees are motivated to identify improvements and changes to existing products and services that will serve to increase customer appeal.
- Employees who are supported and engaged will be better prepared and motivated to meet the timely needs of customers.
- More nimble business processes developed and managed by employees (facilitated by management) will result in the increased speed by which customers' needs can be satisfied.
- Employees who are happy and motivated will be more apt to manage your social presence and support the continued improvement of your company brand.

Consider that on a daily basis it's your employees who have the ability to "touch" your customers, either through one-on-one interactions or though the products or services that they participate in the creation and delivery of. Are you and your leadership team investing time and energy creating a stronger connection between your employees and customers? Moreover, are your employees empowered to take action to ensure that your customers receive perpetual value from your products and services that they might come to expect?

Connecting employees with customers is not the only external business relationship that adds value and supports a more empowered operation. Suppliers, contractors, and other external resources offer significant insight into improved processes, products, services, and competitive opportunities that can support a more efficient and effective operation. In Chapter 8, I will discuss how suppliers are an untapped resource for most companies, and how you can tap into this resource to support more effective and innovative operations within your organization.

8

One Big Happy Family

Suppliers, Your Untapped Resource

There are few businesses that operate without the support of an external supplier, contractor, or resource. Even a service-based business like mine relies on various subcontractors in order to support daily operations, including accounting, website, and social media support. When you consider this, it's no wonder that the field of supply chain management has become increasingly valued as a contributor to organizational effectiveness during the past two decades.

During my career, I have spent some time in supply chain management, overseeing areas that included inventory management, logistics, and strategic sourcing. As my career progressed into more operation and project-focused roles, it became apparent that the challenge within the field of supply chain management is in the understanding and application of the "management" aspect itself. Let me give you a brief example. If you speak with companies that directly or indirectly provide products to Walmart, you will be able to clearly identify two underlying messages. They are happy with the high volume of goods that they sell, but they are unhappy with the near ridiculous demands that are placed on them in the form of continuously reducing cost from their products, and navigating logistical requirements and often extended terms that place undue and challenging requirements on the supplier. Walmart focuses heavily on managing their suppliers. This means that collaboration is not its first priority, instead choosing to manage its suppliers to fit within predetermined criteria. I predict that Walmart as we know it today will no longer exist in the next two decades by the way, and for good reason. Companies like JD.com and Amazon, two of the world's largest online retailers, continue to evolve their business model allowing them to distribute everything from books to fresh food to car parts, all directly to the door of consumers. As consumers become accustomed to this level of service, there will no longer be the same demand for a retail presence, thus reducing revenue for Walmart and in turn making the overhead to sustain Walmart's existing brick-and-mortar infrastructure impossible. Do you think its suppliers will be lined up to provide further financial support and incentives to help Walmart navigate this difficult position? The answer is no. They will have little profit margin and little incentive to do so.

There is a better way.

Treating a supplier as a cherished partner, a resource that will support continued business evolution, is the only way to ensure that your company will survive and thrive in the decades ahead. If you want to see a great example of a more collaborative approach, consider the military. As a sector with considerable spending power, the military relies on and encourages innovation and collaboration with its suppliers, and for good reason. Without the support of suppliers to produce the vehicles, weapons, and technology to protect our country, there in fact would be no military, only men and women ready to serve. This isn't to say that downward pressure on pricing is lacking for suppliers to the military sector; however, it does demonstrate a viable and valuable approach to collaborating with suppliers. Many of Walmart's initiatives, on the other hand, such as its desire for greater control of inbound transportation from suppliers and its earlier failed RFID mandate,[1] have been the result of internal initiatives at Walmart, rather than a focus on external collaboration with suppliers.

In this chapter we will discuss how collaboration between suppliers and their customers is not as rampant or prevalent as you might think. Despite the recognition by most CEOs and executives of the value that suppliers and contractors can offer to a business, the reality is that the continued introduction and use of one-sided negotiation tools such as competitive bidding and e-auctions, as well as cost-focused initiatives that favor the company more than the supplier, in effect reduce the ability and willingness of suppliers to support and participate in collaborative relationships.

Why Focusing on Price Kills Supplier Collaboration

A couple of years ago I was facilitating a session with a group of senior leaders from the Canadian public sector, many of whom had worked for a government agency for at least a decade. Our discussions were around how to increase the value obtained from supplier relationships, while still mitigating and managing price increases and overruns. As the morning progressed, the tension within the room grew. These leaders, although in agreement with the ideas we were discussing, grew continuously uncomfortable with how they might put the ideas we discussed into practice. Sensing their growing concerns, I asked, "What's stopping you from moving forward with some of these ideas?" The room went silent until an individual stepped forward and suggested that existing policies made it difficult to collaborate with suppliers. More specifically, there were policies that governed the decisions and actions of those whose job it was to source and select suppliers and contractors that the lowest price bid should win in virtually every instance. Although created out of the right intent, to ensure that the government minimizes spending, the introduction of such policy eliminates the ability to collaborate with suppliers and ultimately directs the award of business to the lowest-priced bidders who typically offer insufficient quality, an inability to achieve projects in a timely manner, and who have a track record of significant and costly project overruns. As we discussed this further, it became clear that virtually every individual in the room felt that the existing policies often forced him or her to select suppliers who, although the lowest cost initially, ended up being the highest cost in the end.

Are your policies supporting or hindering supplier collaboration?

Companies that empower their operations for greater effectiveness focus less intently on managing price, and place a greater emphasis on the value they obtain from the relationship. A focus solely on price results in a lose-lose scenario, as it drives obstacles between the buyer and seller relationship that reduce collaboration and support an environment of ill feelings and distrust.

The idea of obtaining a competitive price for products and services makes complete sense, with the objective to minimize a supplier or contractor's profit margin to something that is deemed reasonable. But what is reasonable? Who should decide what a reasonable price is? The answer is the marketplace; however, by focusing solely on obtaining the "best" price (which is often the lowest price), we often circumvent the profitability that the supplier has decided is necessary in order to remain viable.

In the automotive industry crisis of 2009–2010, dozens of automotive suppliers closed their doors as a result of either bankruptcy or lack of profitability.[2] With little volume, increased demands from OEM companies, and minimal profit margins (having been squeezed by the OEMs for continued price reductions throughout the previous decade), there was little choice for many companies that supported the automotive industry other than to shut down their operations, leaving OEMs scrambling to find alternate sources of supply. These challenges are not limited to the automotive sector alone.

Focusing solely on price diminishes a buyer-supplier relationship from one of sharing and collaboration to one that hinges on price. The more you squeeze, the less you get. It's no different from visiting a discount grocery chain store rather than a traditional store. There are no frills, and that typically also means that there is a smaller selection of food options to choose from, there are no bags or bagging services for your groceries, there aren't any conveniences like a public washroom, and most of the shelf-life products are nearing their expiration date.

You get what you pay for.

If this is the case, then why do we continue to train and educate our engineers and supply chain professionals to focus on getting the best price? A better approach is to focus on obtaining value that hinges on collaboration surrounding price, allowing the supplier and buyer to reach an agreement on what is reasonable. This means that tools such as reverse auctions and hard-line negotiations must be a thing of the past. Don't get me wrong, I'm a proponent of obtaining a fair price, but I also don't want to squeeze a supplier to the point of any of the following:

1. The supplier lacks financial viability or worse yet faces possible bankruptcy.
2. The quality of the product or service the supplier provides is diminished relative to my needs or expectations.
3. The supplier substitutes an alternate product that is of lower quality or characteristics than I require.
4. The supplier redirects costs to alternate areas that are less obvious to me, thereby skewing actual costs.
5. The supplier engages in unethical practices such as providing counterfeit products.
6. The supplier is forced to change how it operates to the extent that it influences any of the areas above.

If any of the points above sound unreasonable to you, or if you're thinking that they can't possibly happen to your company with existing suppliers, think again. Personally, in my experience of working in the supply chain, I can tell you that I have encountered situations in which any or all of these circumstances exist, and if it can happen to these companies, then it can happen to your company.

The most empowered and profitable companies place price as a tertiary focus area, not a primary focus in operating their businesses. They recognize that in most instances you get what you pay for; hence higher investments often result in higher rewards, and the ability to obtain products and services that set them apart from their competition and help them hold a competitive advantage in the marketplace.

Companies with an empowered and effective operation place their focus on creating close connections between internal working groups such as operations, supply chain, and engineering with customer-facing work groups such as marketing, sales, and customer service in order to ensure customer feedback and intelligence is shared and contrasted against supplier challenges and opportunities. This changes the focus from how cheaply a product or service can be made or purchased to what truly matters, which is providing products and services that the customer expects and is willing to pay for—products and services that add value.

At Bellwyck Packaging there is constant interaction between purchasing and sales, and has been for over a decade. The president, Jeff Sziklai, recognizes that all employees must have a connection with the customer to understand what it is that they are striving to achieve and to ensure that finance (which includes supply chain), production (which includes manufacturing and other support services), customer service, and sales all connect on a regular basis in a face-to-face setting to share customer feedback and intelligence, as well as supplier challenges and innovations. Through these forums, focus on price becomes less prevalent, replaced by the desire to produce and deliver what customers need and value.

Generally speaking, people expect to get what they pay for. When was the last time you heard someone brag about how cheaply his or her car was built, or how poorly constructed his or her smartphone was? The answer is never. It's critical for companies to place less emphasis on price and put more effort into ensuring that all employees and in turn suppliers understand clearly and support what it is that their customers value.

Finding Value in Supplier Collaboration

In forming a closer connection between an organization and its suppliers, companies are positioned to reap the rewards of supplier collaboration. Attention turns away from finding the lowest possible price and toward finding ideal and innovative solutions to achieve market distinction and dominance. You can test how well you are using supplier collaboration to achieve market distinction today by using the following approach (Figure 8.1).

Figure 8.1 Achieve Market Distinction

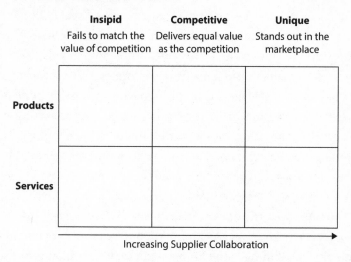

	Insipid	Competitive	Unique
	Fails to match the value of competition	Delivers equal value as the competition	Stands out in the marketplace
Products			
Services			

Increasing Supplier Collaboration ⟶

I mentioned earlier in this chapter that collaboration with external suppliers and contractors is not as rampant as you might think. Let me explain why. In most businesses, there is a gatekeeper that any supplier, contractor, consultant, or external resource must first work with before ever being considered for offering products or services to a company. Invariably, this is someone at the front lines of the business, working in purchasing or finance, who typically sees himself or herself as the gatekeeper and is proud of the title. Such people pride themselves in "keeping out the riff-raff," but the problem is that they are neither trained nor knowledgeable in recognizing what value that external resource might offer.

I sometimes fall into this trap in my own business. Several years ago, the president of a large association approached me at an event where he had heard me speak and said, "Shawn, you would be a great facilitator for our strategic retreat this year. Can you assist us with forming our renewed strategy?"

After a brief discussion, the president suggested that I speak with John, the man who was organizing the event, and provide him with a proposal. What happened following this discussion is what almost always happens with providers of products and services each and every day—the president asked me to work with someone in charge of arranging the event, not someone who understood the unique and diverse needs of the association board or who had the ability to judge the performance and value of the services. In essence, John was good at finding a facility and arranging lunch, but not good at what was necessary to make a valuable outcome from the strategy retreat. Recognizing this to be the case, I suggested that I follow up with the president after speaking with John, to which the president agreed. After making several unsuccessful attempts to connect with John, I returned to the president and we formalized a proposal for me to facilitate the retreat. "I guess John was too busy," suggested the president.

"Yes, it appears that way," was my response.

How many opportunities is your business missing out on because your gatekeepers treat every supplier, contractor, or consultant as a commodity? Obtaining value from supplier collaboration is not something that can be delegated down to those who don't understand what value is desired or even necessary. Empowered operations that collaborate with suppliers and other external resources allow the internal subject matter experts with decision-making authority to have the ability to engage in the collaboration process.

There are eight ways that collaborating with suppliers can offer value to a business or association:

1. **New ideas or innovations.** Companies such as Procter & Gamble have built their business on strong external supplier collaboration through platforms such as "Open Innovation," a P&G program that allows external inventors to partner with P&G to bring new products to the marketplace.

2. **Increased transparency.** In collaborative relationships (rather than the historically price-focused adversarial relationships), there is a greater willingness to be transparent about costs and overhead. Through transparency, opportunities arise to partner on new ways to produce and supply products in order to reduce costs and share in revenue increases.

3. **Increased skill and knowledge.** Through collaboration, there is a greater willingness and ability to share the skills and knowledge of

supplier resources and company resources. It wasn't until the parent company Merck presented Xirallic, a chemical that produces a rainbow of colors in today's metallic paints,[3] to many of the recognized automotive brands of today like Ford, Nissan, and Toyota that the enhanced metallic in today's automotive paints became commonplace.

4. **Increased speed to market.** Through collaboration there is a greater ability and willingness to share information that pertains to producing or delivering products and services to the market. This ability results in being able to deliver new products and services to the market faster than if done without supplier support. When Steve Jobs was attempting to bring iTunes to the market, he focused on collaborating with powerful figures such as Paul Vidich, a then vice president at Warner. Steve recognized that in order to quickly and successfully bring iTunes to the market he would first have to form strong collaborative partnerships with the key players,

5. **Shared risk.** Early in my career, while leading a supply chain team, I was approached by a supplier who asked if they might obtain access to our database allowing them to scrub the data and make numerous corrections. They explained that our data was corrupt, resulting in numerous duplications that in turn cost them time resolving for each and every order they received. Their intent was simple. Scrub only the data that was for their specific part numbers, and then return to us for uploading. Their efforts would be at no cost and would in the end help both companies to increase the accuracy and speed of purchases. There were risks of course. Despite the supplier's investment of time and energy we might source the products from another supplier, eliminating any ROI they might experience in having a clean database from which their products were identified. There were also risks for our company in allowing an external source access to our database. In the end the project was concluded and provided significant benefits to both parties in the term of faster quotation response time and a reduction in the number of incorrect

product returns. Shared risk through collaboration often results in shared rewards.

6. **Streamline processes.** In a collaborative supplier relationship, there is greater visibility and awareness of exactly what it takes for the supplier to provide a product or service and the urgency by which it is needed by the buyer. This creates visibility to opportunities to improve existing business processes both between the buyer and seller and as internal to each party in order to reduce lead times and reduce costs.

7. **Revenue enhancement.** In a collaborative relationship where there is a greater willingness to be transparent relative to costs and an ability to recognize and resolve process bottlenecks or delays, there is naturally an opportunity to collectively increase revenue. By sharing in revenue enhancement opportunities, both parties are increasingly open to share further information to continue to reduce costs and increased speed to market.

8. **Increased visibility.** The more information is shared between a buyer and supplier or contractor, the greater the visibility into the value chain. If, for example, you were to learn (or think consciously about) the fact that in order for you to eat strawberries in the winter months they must be sourced and shipped from Turkey, Spain, or even Egypt, would you be as surprised that prices are as high as they are today? Likely not. The more information that is known about the value chain, the greater the opportunity to collectively discuss what is valuable and what is not, leading to new ideas, cost alternatives, and changes in customer education.

Ultimately there is significantly greater value in collaborating with suppliers than there is in focusing solely on price, service, and quality. It is important to mention, however, that not every supplier relationship should be collaborative. There simply isn't value in every relationship, nor should there be. With this in mind, let's discuss how to introduce supplier collaboration in order to achieve the greatest value for your business and your customers.

Introducing Supplier Collaboration

There are examples of supplier collaboration all around us. These are predominantly in areas where the following factors exist:

1. It is considered "safe" to hand over responsibility of a product or service and its management to an outside resource.
2. The complexity or knowledge required to manage the product or service is deemed too costly or involved for a business or association to invest in. It's deemed easier to tap into the knowledge of an expert who spends his entire career focused on remaining current and up-to-date to specialize in the product or service in question.

Here are a few examples of collaborative support services that you may be familiar with or your organization might use:

Management of events. A colleague of mine, David Jewell, provides a unique service to associations and nonprofits in sourcing and finding the best venues for events. His extensive knowledge of the event industry allows him to remain current on the value that various venues offer, and he is the most educated when it comes to helping connect association events with preferred venues.

Management of inventory. Another colleague of mine is Tim Cox, president of KC Distribution, an industrial supply company. Tim not only offers a wide range of competitive products and services to his industrial clients, but also a service whereby he will deliver and even support the management of on-site inventory, allowing his clients the opportunity to reduce their investment in both the cost of managing inventory and the overhead required to purchase and store inventory.

Management of communications. Lisa Larter is a close friend and colleague whom I've known for years. Lisa is an expert in social media and has been offering social media management to corporate companies for nearly a decade. In an age when information is the key to managing a company brand and increasing awareness of the value a product or service can offer, Lisa helps her corporate clients gain recognition of their products and services, expanding their reach to a broader audience and engaging younger buyers who spend the predominance of their time online.

Management of logistics. Eddie Rei is the president of Triumph Express Service Canada, a provider who specializes in managing logistics into North America from Asia. Eddie's company handles all of the steps in the transaction, from sourcing the most cost-effective and reliable carriers to completing all necessary customs transactions in an accurate and timely manner. With the continued growth of exports from Asia, Eddie's company offers peace of mind at a competitive price for manufacturers in the North American market.

Digital brand management. I've been working with Chad Barr, of the Chad Barr Group, for several years. Chad helps entrepreneurs and business owners build a global digital empire in order to expand their marketing reach and deliver value to their clients and customers. Having spent over two decades building websites, online applications (apps), and social media presence, Chad and his team are able to help business owners successfully portray a professional image that is both distinct and attractive to their customers.

These are just a few examples that come to mind. For a service or product to be successful in every instance above, there must be a collaborative relationship in play. Referring to the example of digital brand management, it would be impossible for Chad and his team to effectively portray the image and value of their clients to the global marketplace if they didn't know and understand their clients' business. Alternatively, it is virtually impossible for an association to identify and source the right venue at the optimum price without employing someone full time, a far greater investment (and a shift away from an association's core competency) than engaging the services of David Jewell.

Supplier collaboration can be integrated much deeper than these common examples, but the right environment must exist in order to form a win-win scenario. Figure 8.2 notes a means to identify those suppliers, contractors, consultants, and other external resources that you should engage in a collaborative relationship. I call this the Collaboration Calculator.

Figure 8.2 Collaboration Calculator

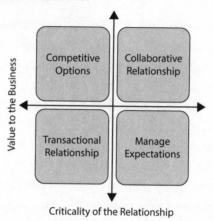

Empowered operations use the Collaboration Calculator or a similar process to contrast the value of new and existing supplier relationships with the business vision and objectives in order to identify where collaboration would provide the greatest value to the business.

Typically, this would entail identifying those suppliers who:

- Are the most critical to providing or producing the company's products or services
- Equate to the largest investment that the business is making in an outside company or resource
- Offer the greatest opportunity to identify and create new customer value
- Provide resources and knowledge that would otherwise be unattainable or too expensive to attain
- Offer a new entry point into an existing market or customer base
- Present an opportunity to create an entry point into a new and untapped market

After the calculator has identified the best and most viable opportunities for collaboration, the next step is to pursue the introduction of collaboration into the relationship. Pursuing the optimal supplier collaboration opportunities results from what I call the Ten Commandments of Collaboration:

1. **Have an open-door policy.** Too many businesses put purchasing and contract management professionals in place to act as the gatekeeper, warding off new suppliers or contractors and tightly managing those that already exist. This is counterintuitive to how you can increase opportunities for collaboration. In order to obtain opportunities (and not insult existing or new suppliers or contractors), it's critical that an open-door policy exists in which new sources of products and services, as well as existing sources, are encouraged to meet with those who may need their new ideas and innovations rather than wait until the gatekeeper decides it's the right time to enter.

2. **Seek out new suppliers.** Just because you have a longstanding relationship with an external resource for your company doesn't mean that you should be unreceptive to new sources or new offerings. I mentioned earlier my relationship with Chad Barr of the Chad Barr Group, which evolved because I was open to speaking with Chad prior to our relationship. Although I had a previous provider for website services, I was always open to speaking with Chad and listening to his ideas. This meant that when my previous website management company began to falter in its service, it was a no-brainer for me to contact Chad and begin a professional relationship. Every company should be receptive to and seek out new relationships.

3. **Understand your needs.** Business is not a crystal ball; it's impossible to be able to make connections with the right sources of collaboration if you aren't clear on what your company, its employees, and its customers truly need and in turn will value. I've seen more businesses sold on integrating an ERP system that in turn added more complexity to their process rather than streamlining it, than I'd care to admit. The reason is that the businesses weren't clear on what they needed before meeting with the supplier to investigate

options. In virtually all of these instances there is a poor relationship between the company and the ERP supplier, and collaboration is virtually nonexistent.

4. **Understand the marketplace.** Referencing my earlier example, I wouldn't have met with Chad if I were not attuned to the opportunities that existed from other web services providers. As Chad's focus is on designing an all-encompassing global digital presence rather than simply a website, his approach and unique service offerings were attractive, which in turn drove the conversation. If I hadn't been receptive to what existed in the marketplace as alternatives or improvements to my existing products or services, this relationship would never have begun.

5. **Pursue and leverage technology.** In the information age, there are more viable opportunities to collaborate with suppliers and contractors than ever before. Advancements in electronic data interchange (EDI) and integration of cloud-based services offer companies the ability to share more information with their suppliers and contractors than ever before. Technology offers the ability to increase collaboration and improve the collaboration that exists.

6. **Study your competition.** One of the greatest means to increase collaboration opportunities is to study your competition. What are your competitors doing to increase collaboration and value to their customers or clients? What are they doing to capitalize on the expertise of external resources? Larsen and Shaw, whom I've mentioned earlier in this book, decided to integrate a fully functional chat module onto their website once conversations turned to realizing that some of the largest competitors had this functionality in place as a means to better serve existing customers and connect with new customers.

7. **Be transparent.** It's virtually impossible to build a collaborative relationship if you aren't first willing to share your needs, opportunities, and challenges. Despite the confidentiality of specifications and needs, the military shares a considerable amount of information and intelligence with its key suppliers, as it realizes

that the equipment it is purchasing must be fit for the intended use. End use and functionality need must be clear if the supplier is going to ensure the military gets what it pays for.

8. **Be receptive to feedback and ideas.** The very idea of having a gatekeeper is problematic because it is virtually impossible for one person to understand the needs of many. During my time working in supply chain management, not only did I create a stronger bond with sales and marketing, but I also spent time visiting with employees on the production floor. Through these visits I was able to remain current on the challenges they were having in efficiently operating equipment and using supplied products and materials. I didn't walk away from complaints about a supplier's quality; I encouraged them. When the supplier came to the site to discuss the issue, I took the opportunity to have the supplier speak with the operator and let the supplier see the problem firsthand. Being open and receptive to employee feedback and involving employees in supplier interactions is key to building more valuable collaborative relationships with suppliers.

9. **Create a collaborative environment.** Several years ago, I assisted a client in organizing an event prior to their supplier conference in which we called in several of their key suppliers. The premise of the meeting was to present to the small group some customer challenges the organization had been facing and to create and facilitate a collaborative forum in which we could interact with the suppliers, and they with each other, on finding potential solutions. Collaboration often does not come naturally. Creating collaboration requires an environment that supports it with intent and purpose.

10. **Share rewards and celebrate successes.** This may seem to be something that would evolve naturally in a collaborative environment, but in my experience that's not the case. In order to entice employees, suppliers, contractors, and other partners to collaborate, there must be incentive, and sometimes the opportunity for more business or higher profits simply isn't enough if the

reward takes longer than the perceived investment of time and resources suggests. Like any successful initiative, it's critical that any and all achieved successes be shared with others internal and external to the company (to convince them that success in such an approach is possible) and to entice those involved to continue their mission to build upon their success with further ideas and opportunities.

Collaboration doesn't come easy, and it doesn't come cheap. It is not something that can be put into place overnight, but instead requires a longstanding commitment to increasing value to customers and collaborative partners alike. This said, there are continued evolutions in supplier collaboration that are worth mentioning to allow you to stay at the forefront of this significant opportunity to further empower your operations.

The Evolution of Supplier Relationships

As I write this, Amazon is seeking Federal Aviation Administration (FAA) approval to deliver packages to the doors of its customers via drones. I can't speak to whether this will inevitably be possible, but it poses the question as to what may be possible in the future that will allow a business to partner closely with its suppliers and other partners in order to form and sustain a powerful competitive advantage. From my research and studies in supplier collaboration, here are some emerging trends to consider as a starting point:

1. **Controlling the customer's experience.** I mentioned how Amazon is seeking to improve its ability to serve customers, but look deeper at what it is doing. Amazon has become a global marketplace that connects buyers and sellers, retailers and consumers alike. It is seeking to introduce drones through collaboration with the FAA, allowing it to create enhanced and safe guidelines for the operation of drones in a controlled airspace, something that is highly regulated today, but for much larger aircraft.

In order to retain its existing customers and continue to attract new customers, Amazon is seeking to takeover the transportation of products from its distribution centers to customers gaining further control over its customers' experience with Amazon. What services and products could your company integrate that would allow for further control over your customers' experience? How might suppliers (existing or potential) support your initiative?

2. **Global knowledge repository.** With the advent and growing integration of web-based services, there is an increased ability on the part of companies both large and small to tap into knowledge instantaneously from around the world. Companies like Elance, Fiverr, and Crowdspring have created platforms that allow any individual or business to tap into the knowledge and creativity of the global marketplace, allowing for fresh perspectives and new ideas.

   We have shifted from using the yellow pages for regional knowledge to tapping into a global community that broadens opportunities for collaboration beyond what we've seen before. How are you tapping into this global knowledge repository to collaborate and increase value to your customers and business?

3. **Digital consumption of information.** For several years I have been sending a weekly newsletter filled with pragmatic ideas and tips on how to improve and empower business performance. The newsletter, which you can access at www.casemoreandco.com, has a readership in the thousands and is a demonstration of how we as human beings are consuming more and more information online.

   This is a somewhat straightforward example of digital consumption. However, if you consider companies such as Second Life (www.secondlife.com), which offer members the chance to build a virtual life that mimics the reality they choose, it becomes increasingly clear that not only are we consuming more information digitally, but we are growing increasingly closer to being able to (and wanting to) build the physical world into a digital one. Are you seeking opportunities to collaborate that will allow your customers, corporate or consumer, to consume digital information and experiences?

These of course are only a few ideas meant to shift your thinking toward *how* you can collaborate with external suppliers and the broader marketplace, thereby increasing the value you offer to your customers, clients, and members, and ultimately to create a more compelling and sustained competitive advantage.

9

Working Toward a Common Goal
Nurturing Internal Collaboration

S o far, we've discussed the power of various sources of external collaboration for a business, both with its customers and suppliers,
but what of internal collaboration? Over a decade ago, I was managing a team of professionals whose role it was to purchase products and
services from suppliers and contractors to the business. Their role,
although important relative to managing company spending, was governed almost solely by engineering. Virtually everything purchased, with
the exception of dispensable items like paper and pencils, was identified, sourced, and qualified by engineering. As engineering was a separate department reporting to a different business unit, there were often
conflicting objectives, referenced in Chapter 3, between our business
unit and engineering. Generally speaking, these professionals were held
accountable to reduce spending and leverage buys, whereas engineering
was expected to find products and solutions that resolved problems or
supported the development of new products or services. Cost for engineering was a secondary factor.

The banter between these groups had been going on for years, so
after working with my team for a few months it became clear that
collaboration was necessary if we were to overcome the conflicting objectives and help both teams recognize that we were all trying
to achieve the same objective—support a high-performing and highly

profitable company. There had been a myriad of solutions attempted over the years, for example:

- Weekly or monthly meetings between the groups
- Discussions between the business unit executives in order to find common ground on objectives
- Projects initiated between the two work groups
- Root cause analysis and other exploratory activities that required engagement between the two groups

I should mention that geographically these groups were situated mere feet from each other, separated only by a few offices.

The lackluster results or downright failure of the solutions outlined above suggested that we needed to take more drastic action in order to build collaboration. For collaboration to occur there must be an ability to interact. We decided to mix up seating arrangements, creating room for several engineers to sit within our group to drive more interaction and discussion. You can imagine the resistance we met once the seating plan had been organized and the idea was proposed to both my team and the engineers, but we decided, in order to minimize conflict, that we would avoid formalizing any interactivity, requiring only that the engineers sit amid my team (they still focused on their own objectives and tasks and reported to their existing manager). The results were astounding.

Within days these individuals were talking, sharing ideas, posing solutions, and educating each other on why decisions were made, driving an increased understanding between the two groups as well as a common bond. Simply by seating these individuals amid each other, we were able to create powerful internal collaboration that minimized conflict and maximized the value and volume of ideas put forth.

Collaboration is not a complex process. It is in essence building a forum in which the whole is more powerful than the sum of its parts. In this chapter I will present a clear case for why nurturing internal collaboration is one of the most significant approaches to creating a competitive advantage, despite whether you are in the manufacturing, distribution, retail, or not-for-profit sector. We will discuss a model that you can employ to build more powerful collaboration, setting your business apart from your competition. Lastly, we will discuss the barriers to building more powerful internal collaboration and how to overcome them within each level of the organization, including:

- Leadership collaboration
- Interdepartmental collaboration
- Cross-departmental collaboration

Capitalize on Collaboration: Setting Your Approach

Let's start by clarifying what internal collaboration is and what it is not, and how selecting the right approach to collaboration can be the difference between achieving your desired results and not. We aren't on a mission to have everyone sit in a circle, hold hands, and sing "Kumbaya." Collaboration is the interactivity of individuals with the sole intent of producing or creating something. Collaborations come in all sizes and can include as few as two individuals or several large groups working together. What is important to consider is that relative to workplace collaboration, the most powerful collaborations are those that involve individuals with varying degrees of knowledge, experience, and ideas. If I were to place two engineers from the same company in a room and ask them to work together to resolve a problem or create a new solution, chances are that the outcome would be more technically focused (with little consideration for how to bring the solution to life) than if I put an engineer and a production manager in the same room with a similar and relevant problem.

In the first instance, the engineers are going to come up with solutions and ideas that are appropriate to their education, background, and knowledge, but if presented to someone who is not an engineer, the solution may seem too detailed or extensive. Put an engineer with someone who will have to bring his or her idea or design to life, and there will be more productive and tangible outcomes. This falls within the Collaboration Calibration dial that I use as a gauge to ascertain the power of internal collaborative discussions.

The Collaboration Calibration dial shows that as diversity of individuals increases, so too does the value, viability, and pragmatism of the solution or end result.

This brings me to a key argument that I want to make about collaboration. An interaction or discussion between two or more people is not true collaboration unless it yields tangible and powerful results. Referring to my earlier example of collaboration, within weeks we began to witness and experience some very tangible and intangible benefits to the new seating arrangement, specifically:

- Reduced volume of e-mails between the two working groups
- A reduced lead time to resolve technical concerns during the procurement process
- Reduction in the backlog of unsanctioned purchases that required technical review and assessment
- More rapid response to production needs requiring technical and procurement cooperation

Without tangible and intangible outcomes, there is no collaboration, only a conversation. This is similar in concept to forming a new strategy: the ideas generated are simply ideas if in fact there are no recognizable or tangible outcomes that result from them. My argument is counterintuitive to what you may have witnessed in the marketplace today, where there are a plethora of technology companies pitching their software as *the tool* to initiate collaboration. If you think purchasing a software solution that provides a platform for interactivity between work groups is a path to collaboration, you're wrong. Go ahead right now and Google the word *collaboration* again. You will find that at least two software companies pop up on the first search page. They want you to believe that through their software you can achieve collaboration. Although there is some relevance to the idea that collaboration must be facilitated and their software may in fact be the ideal solution to do so, the facilitation in itself is only one component of the solution. When you consider my earlier example of collaboration, it may appear that simply by seating individuals from different working groups together we were able to achieve collaboration. This would only be partially true. There were several steps that we moved through in order to prepare for and capitalize on collaboration in this instance (more on this shortly). The key to ensuring that we achieved rapid and valuable outcomes from the collaboration was in first selecting the best approach based on the circumstances, environment, and individuals involved. This is similar to baking cookies. There are dozens, if not hundreds, of recipes out there for chocolate chip cookies, the majority of which would satisfy any palette. Each recipe, although containing similar ingredients, can provide a very different product. In order to determine the best recipe, we first consider our desired outcomes. Are you seeking a cookie that remains soft even after being refrigerated? Are you seeking a cookie that is hard and crumbles? What is the proportion of chocolate chips to the surface area of each cookie? Okay, I may be going a bit far here, but what I want to demonstrate is that collaboration is not a blanket applied to any situation. There are in fact distinct approaches that must be considered in order to ensure the outcome is as you intend.

There are three predominant approaches to internal collaboration, each resulting in different outcomes dependent on the participants and the environment.

1. **Affiliative collaboration.** This is collaboration in which the participating individuals or groups are united in the interests or actions. An example of affiliative collaboration would be a group of engineers working in collaboration to solve a production or quality problem.
   When used: Seeking to find new ideas or form new solutions among an existing or complementary work group.
2. **Evaluative collaboration.** This is collaboration in which participating individuals or groups operate under similar objectives and goals but have opposing views and experiences relative to achieving these goals. The example I described above where the engineer

and procurement professionals were placed in a collaborative environment is an example of evaluative collaboration.

When used: Seeking new ideas or solutions among individuals or working groups who are working within the same organization or business unit and whose roles or daily responsibilities vary but whose overarching objectives in support of a common environment (i.e., business) are aligned.

3. **Conflictive collaboration.** This is collaboration in which those participating are in direct conflict with one another relative to objectives, goals, experiences, and knowledge. If you've ever seen the classic film *Twelve Angry Men*, then you've experienced an example of conflictive collaboration. Internally to a business you often find examples of conflictive collaboration between different business units or between senior management and employees.

When used: Seeking new ideas or solutions among individuals or working groups that have opposing views, objectives, and goals and whose roles or daily responsibilities vary.

The key to ensuring valuable and tangible results from collaboration is ensuring that the right approach is selected and enabled based on the outcomes desired. By understanding these forms of collaboration, it becomes clear as to when and what tools are necessary to ensure that collaboration is both valuable and powerful.

Before we move to discuss a model for forming and capitalizing on internal collaboration, I wanted to touch on a final point. As a frequent speaker for executive forums such as TEC and Vistage, it's not uncommon following my delivering a talk on forming internal collaboration that the president or CEO from an organization will approach me, thank me for the ideas we've discussed, and then ask how they might get their leadership team to collaborate more often. Collaboration is not something that can be enticed; it must be purposefully and strategically integrated. More specifically, collaboration is a tool that if employed correctly can yield more powerful ideas, solutions, and products that meet the needs of today's unpredictable customer. My response when I receive this question is quite simple. I ask the president, as a member to an executive forum, such as Vistage, if he or she finds the interaction with peers valuable, to which the answer is almost always a resounding yes. More specifically, the response usually is that he or she is able to receive valuable feedback on new ideas that can be introduced in any business to increase success, and often as well further validation of their existing thoughts relative to dealing with challenging situations. I reply, "What you've been experiencing and describing here is collaboration in its truest form." After a brief pause I then comment, "I would guess that this collaboration doesn't naturally occur. You put time and energy into achieving these valuable outcomes. Since your business is likely the most important priority in your life next to your family and friends, does it not stand to reason that to achieve similar outcomes from internal collaboration you must lead the charge and put similar energy and time into forming internal collaboration?" Silence generally follows.

If your company is not placing a significant effort into forming collaboration, then you are missing out on the opportunity to generate more creative and tangible solutions to your existing and future challenges. This is not a task to be delegated down, but an approach to unlocking the potential that exists within the business.

The Collaborative Approach: What It Takes to Make It Happen!

There are a plethora of examples of successful business collaborations, such as those between Coca-Cola and Heinz to make more sustainable containers, between NASA and Lego to use Lego as an educational tool to promote technology, mathematics, and engineering among science students, and between Mercedes-Benz and Facebook to create an application that allows drivers to access Facebook from their cars. However, examples of powerful and successful internal collaborations are not as prominent. A likely reason may be that there is less reason to "promote" the collaboration publicly in order to satisfy or excite shareholders as in the examples above. From my consulting work, I can provide you a series of examples where internal collaboration was formed and resulted in powerful outcomes that, although painfully obvious to some, were never going to be realized if the collaboration wasn't strategically formed.

As I mentioned earlier in this book, one of the tools I employ in my consulting work relative to improving operational value is Lean. A couple of years ago, I was asked by Barbara Zeins, president of Gerson and Gerson, to help her improve the speed and accuracy of work flow through the company's garment sewing process. We identified individuals that would be part of the Lean initiative that satisfied two of the three forms of collaboration, namely affiliative and evaluative. The reason we selected individuals who met more than one of these areas was threefold:

1. We wanted those with experience in the working area to be part of the initiative in order to educate others on idiosyncrasies and necessities of the work.
2. We wanted to include other employees who, although they worked for the same company, were able to contribute as internal customers or observers of the work area's performance.
3. As this wasn't an externally facing process (directly impacting the customer), we felt little need to include representatives who fell under the conflictive collaboration form, although we did prepare some individuals such as external customers and suppliers to be "on call" in the event that they were needed.

Over the period of a week, we dissected the entire process relative to how garments were sewn, including all elements of interaction and communication. With the focus on maximizing operational value to the company (rapid completion of sewn garments that met first-pass quality criteria), the team collaborated to identify a more efficient process that met the needs of the various collaborative partners. The results from this event, both tangible and intangible, were powerful.

1. Garments could be sewn faster.
2. Status of garments became easily recognizable for internal customers.
3. Lead times for garments being sewn became more predictable.

4. Increases in the speed of the sewing process reduced the necessity for overtime.
5. A renewed appreciation for the effort required to sew a garment was experienced by all involved.

Internal collaborations are powerful when the right approach, environment, and tools are employed—which brings us to the critical question: how can I make it happen? Collaboration in its truest of forms is built on the five Fs:

1. **Focus.** Formulate clear objectives that have a meaning to participants and show the need to collaborate on solutions. About a year ago, I did some leadership development work with a business unit within a large automotive OEM. The executives leading the group had set stretch goals for their managers that were highly unrealistic based on past performance and the existing work environment. For example, to reduce customer complaints from 11 percent to 2.5 percent of total customer inquiries. Their purpose for setting such "unrealistic" goals was to drive managers to interact both with their teams and with other managers and their teams in order to find "out of the box" solutions. The focus was always the same for all departments: find ways to be more competitive and to drive down costs. Collaboration is built on a shared and clear focus.

2. **Forum.** Collaboration in and of itself takes time and must be presented in the right environment if the results are going to be fruitful. In the example above, managers had been given time individually to digest their objectives and discuss them with team members, following which they were taken off-site for several days with their peers and senior managers to further explore ideas that would support the achievement of their objectives. In addition to time and environment, the right tools are critical to success. Lean, as I described before, is a tool in which employees collaborate in order to define more efficient value-based processes. The underlying support of leaders within a business is also a tool that can serve to support the formation of collaboration. In the example

we discussed earlier, when engineering moved their office locations to sit amid procurement professionals, it took the aligned vision and confidence in the value that would be obtained from the seating arrangements to ensure that we could support the collaboration.

3. **Facilitation.** Collaboration is powerful, but power does not come easy. During the process of collaboration, it's not uncommon to experience personal emotions and reach loggerheads on issues. It's for this reason that simply placing individuals in a room and providing them with tools for collaboration is not enough. There must be some degree of facilitation. We are all humans, and as such we have our own opinions and passions. Effective facilitation ensures that collaboration progresses by helping participants work through emotional issues and overcome loggerheads through compromise. Refer back to my example earlier of Gerson and Gerson. Had I not been there to facilitate the discussions, there is a good chance that the conversations would have not remained focused on the objectives at hand.

4. **Facts.** There is nothing more detrimental to achieving collaboration than conjecture or misconstrued information. I'm not suggesting that someone would purposefully lie when attempting to collaborate with others, but we've all experienced the impact of information that, although we believed it was correct or true, was found to be false. In all collaborations, information must be validated and clearly understood in order to ensure that ideas, outcomes, and recommendations are accurate and achievable. In addition, true collaboration is built on trust, and trust only comes from ensuring that information presented is validated, presented, and perceived in the right light. Ideas, opinions, and beliefs can be validated or revoked through facts and evidence.

5. **Fruition.** Ideas and solutions that are identified through a collaborative approach are highly valuable, but only if they are brought to fruition. With the right forum, focus, and validated facts in place, solutions naturally evolve. With their evolution comes the

necessity to base them in reality. At this point, through the questions of "How will we bring this to life?" or "How do you suggest we go about this?" plans can be formed to bring ideas to life.

McKenna Distribution, run by Steve McKenna and originally run by his father, is a great example of a company that capitalizes on internal collaboration. Steve has taken a highly collaborative approach to engaging with employees, leaders, and even business partners in order to build a thriving and rapidly expanding flooring distribution company. When new challenges or opportunities arise, Steve doesn't take it solely upon himself to solve problems, but engages others to bring new perspectives and effective solutions.

As the business has grown rapidly, Steve has engaged with various employees to ensure customer responsiveness and market competitiveness remain at the forefront of decisions. As Steve brought on new lines and products to serve customers, he recognized that inventory accuracy was critical to long-term success. Through engaging with his controller, CFO, accounts payable, and shipping departments, they realized that several measures were necessary to improve and sustain inventory accuracy. Following our work together and collaboration with his staff, Steve introduced new and more highly intensive inventory cycle counting processes, and supported the development of new reporting to ensure that inventory remained a focal point of the daily operation. Through these collaborative discussions Steve and his team employed a more robust solution through collaborative means.

Building a Business with a Foundation in Collaboration

Within every organization, three significant factors form the foundation of collaboration, specifically from a human capital standpoint, regardless of title or tenure, as identified in Figure 9.1. It is only at the intersection of all three factors that true collaboration can be formed.

Figure 9.1 Collaborative Business Foundation

Explanation of the Collaborative Business Foundation:
Diversity of opinion + Knowledge and experience (but no emotional needs) =
Individual ideas with no passion
Knowledge and experience + Emotional needs (but no diversity of opinion) =
Collective agreement with no innovation
Emotional needs + Diversity of opinion (but no knowledge and experience) =
Incorrect hypothesis

It is only where these three factors intersect, at the point at which emotional needs of employees, diversity of opinion, and knowledge and experience collide, that collaboration flourishes. To deduce whether these three factors exist in your business today, consider the following questions:

1. Are senior leaders aligned in the objectives of the business? Can they recite them in their sleep, and can they explain how every department plays a role in achieving the objectives?
2. Do senior leaders share ideas and challenges openly and seek support from employees and peers in their resolution?
3. Do middle managers and frontline leaders recognize and impact the needs of the business, the leadership team, and the employees?
4. Do middle managers and frontline leaders actively engage across all three levels above to identify and enable solutions to existing challenges or opportunities?
5. Are employees cognizant of the value that diversity within the workforce brings? Can they explain this clearly to anyone who inquires?

6. Do employees capitalize on the experience and knowledge of others in order to consider solutions and options that may not have otherwise been proposed?
7. Are employees willing to connect with others outside their work group in order to tap into a broader network of knowledge and experience?
8. Are the individual emotional needs of employees recognized and supported by all levels of management (including senior leadership)?
9. Is the company actively seeking to increase the diversity of opinion across the organization, tapping into the various generations and levels of experience to find solutions to achieve business objectives?
10. Do all employees understand their individual and collective needs and how their collective experience is more powerful than that of any one individual?

If you answer No to more than one of these questions, then you are failing to create the collaboration necessary to resolve and overcome the greatest challenges your business is facing today, and will be facing tomorrow.

Companies that embrace internal collaboration do so by continuously examining their ability to connect and capitalize on the diversity, knowledge, and needs of their employees. In fact, this is fundamental to how some of the best businesses operate.

Mary Jane Bushell, president and CEO of Larsen and Shaw, focuses much of her attention today on creating more powerful collaborations within her company, realizing that it's through the diversity, knowledge, and experience of the workforce, as well as meeting individual employee needs, that Larsen and Shaw will thrive in the decades to come. Not only has she placed considerable effort into identifying the key components in each of these areas, but she finds herself continuously including, discussing, and promoting these three areas.

Diversity of Opinion

Since taking over as president of the business over two years ago, Mary Jane has placed a concerted effort on attracting and retaining new talent. As a longstanding employer in a small community, Larsen and Shaw has had the benefit of low turnover of staff, with dozens of employees having spent decades working in the company, many of whom have stayed in the same roles. This type of retention and stability comes with both positive and challenging attributes. The employees have a wealth of knowledge in running the operation, but with many facing retirement in the coming years, Mary Jane and her team, has had to focus on attracting and retaining numerous younger-generation employees. With a cross-section of long-term and short-term employees, significant effort has been placed on helping to connect these two generations of employees with the intent of creating more diversity in opinion. "Although we have become very good at what we do, there is always value in a new or fresh perspective."

Knowledge and Experience

With a continuum of new employees entering the workforce and a plethora of longstanding employees retiring, Mary Jane has been faced with a knowledge crunch. How to collect information that is contained in the hearts and minds of longstanding employees and inject this into the younger or newer employees while respecting the needs and desires of both has been a challenge. As a starting point, Mary Jane worked with leaders in the company to identify all of the necessary skills required for roles within the company, from soft skills like leadership to job-specific skills like press setup operation. With the training documented, her team worked to identify the necessary training tools using a combination of online, classroom, and mentorship to ensure all critical skill areas were captured for each employee. Lastly, the information was collected and documented in the company's ERP system as a means of tracking progress and measuring results from the effort. With this information in hand, not only is knowledge and experience for each role recognized, but also new insights relative to employee education, background, and training have come to light, providing insights into further employee deployment in other areas of the business.

Employee Needs

Several years ago John, then president of Larsen and Shaw, along with Mary Jane and the leadership team underwent a powerful team-building event, during which all of the employees were charged with identifying their "Why." This interaction led to the development of a document that encapsulated why employees enjoyed working at Larsen and Shaw, why they stayed, and why they told others it was a great place to work. The insights from these sessions provided intelligence that had no shelf life, as it pertained to ideas and opportunities to further enhance employee motivation and job satisfaction. During the formulation of their strategy, I worked with Mary Jane and her team to connect this "Why" with the purpose of their strategy. This formulated the basis for why the strategy was important not just to senior leadership, but to all of the employees who supported the business. To motivate employees, it's critical that you first understand why they come to work each and every day.

Mary Jane prides herself on having a collaborative team both at the senior leadership level and across the business: "Collaboration is the key to everything we do; it helps us bring more powerful solutions to bear that will see us into a strong and prosperous future."

If you are like most executives, the idea of collaboration is not new. In fact, you've likely used it a time or two when it comes to your business, your employees, or your leadership team. Like most, however, the pursuit of collaboration can appear less than fruitful if you come across significant barriers to its attainment. Before we go any further, it's important that we take a moment to identify those barriers and how we can overcome them in order to achieve value from our collaboration efforts.

Barriers to Collaboration: Don't Let Unforeseen Obstacles Distract You

I would be remiss if I didn't discuss some of the obstacles that you are likely to come across when initiating or pursuing collaboration. Some of these challenges are quite common and can easily be overcome, whereas others are not as common and can be considerably more complex to surmount. I've compiled a list of the most common obstacles that any business leader will face when pursuing and sustaining collaboration, with ideas for overcoming each obstacle based on my experiences with clients from around North America.

1. **Inability to clearly communicate objectives.** Without the ability to clearly state and gain understanding on business objectives, there is little chance collaboration will be possible. This typically occurs in businesses where the vision or strategy for the future is either nonexistent or only in written form (most often contained in a secret binder in the president's office). If the vision for the future of the organization, or the objectives necessary to achieve the vision, is unknown or unclear, it's highly unlikely that there will be open collaboration. To gain buy-in to objectives, it's critical that objectives are clear, present, and known by everyone. This provides the foundation upon which decisions are based and measured.

   How to overcome: Ensure that the vision is clearly communicated in a form that has meaning to all employees, not just leadership (refer to Chapter 2). Consistently communicate objectives, challenges, and opportunities the company is facing to engage employees at all levels in identifying solutions to tackle the most challenging business opportunities that you're facing.

2. **Inability to overcome individual differences.** Within every company there are individual differences. These can exist at all levels, from the board and senior leadership all the way down to employees on the front lines. We are all unique and different, resulting in differing opinions and views. The challenge (in fact the opportunity) is in helping others recognize the value our individual differences bring to the table.

   How to overcome: True collaboration requires facilitation (as I discussed earlier) in order to bring awareness to the value in these differences, as well as to be sure differences are surmounted, not succumbed to. Promote the value of differences and use facilitation as a means to overcome these obstacles.

3. **Failure to capture any perceivably valuable ideas.** During a recent talk to a group of CEOs, someone said, "Shawn, this sounds

fine, but to be honest we tried to facilitate collaboration around a few different business challenges we were facing, only to find that the ideas generated were completely unrealistic. They always seemed to turn toward hiring more people or buying new equipment." This isn't an uncommon problem. In fact, rarely have I facilitated a collaborative session where these challenges didn't arise; however, the key is in how the collaboration is organized. For example, consider a typical problem that any business might face such as a cash crunch. Accounts receivable isn't keeping up with accounts payable, and as a result new ideas need to be found. *How to overcome:* Start by setting ground rules for the collaboration, such as discussing:

- What you've tried in the past and why it hasn't worked.
- What ideas should not be considered as they are unrealistic at the present time (e.g., hiring more people).
- What unorthodox ideas competitors or other industries might have applied to similar challenges.
- Ideas must be tangible, meaning that the group must be able to develop tangible plans to their realization.

4. **Inability to agree on tactics to bring ideas to life.** Another objection I get frequently is that time and money invested in collaboration does not deliver the return that was initially expected. Lean is a great example of this. Most companies have heard of Lean and integrated its practices to some extent; however, in some instances Lean can seem like a "make-work" project, the costs of which can outweigh the initial recognized and quantifiable benefits (when you consider bringing in facilitators, ongoing training, training materials, supporting change initiatives, etc.).
   How to overcome: Work together to clearly define and agree upon objectives and the milestones and measures that will identify when you are on your way to achieving success and when you've reached your desired destination. With objectives agreed upon, the way by which success is achieved is less important than achieving success itself.

5. **Lack of support.** "I've tried to get my senior leadership team to buy into collaboration, but they don't seem to get it (or don't want to get it)" is another comment I hear from CEOs all too frequently. Collaboration requires all hands on deck, to put it lightly. It cannot be forced or instilled in people, and hence it can't be treated as a program or approach in itself. One of the ways I've helped clients move to a more collaborative work environment is through the use of various approaches such as self-managed teams (to eliminate managerial overhead and provide more autonomy to employees), Lean kaizen events (to support collaborative group decision making around increasing value to customers), and hoshin kanri strategy deployment (to support communication and collaborative strategy deployment).

   How to overcome: The key is to think of collaboration not as a means to an end in itself, but as an approach to building a stronger, more powerful connection across the organization to increase productivity and value of interactions.

6. **Lack of fluidity in collaboration roles.** Collaboration requires fluidity in roles. Specifically, there are no hats to be worn; everyone is treated as an equal. This is a challenge for many, particularly those in leadership roles who are accustomed to making decisions and taking action. But if these habits become present in collaboration, the result is participants returning to their historic roles, believing that the desire to be collaborative was only a front for some other plan.

   How to overcome: For any collaboration to be effective, the key is to ensure that all involved recognize the value that each brings to the table, and in turn are open to sharing, considering, and supporting the ideas of others. Referring to my example earlier of Lean, in most kaizen events senior leadership are not even allowed to participate in order to avoid any misperceptions around fluidity in roles.

By considering these challenges and options for their resolution in advance, collaboration can be significantly more powerful and sustainable, offering a more robust and embraced approach to decisions and actions supporting long-term business viability.

With collaboration firmly in place, the opportunity then exists to introduce and capitalize on solutions and ideas that might not have otherwise emerged. This is the point at which innovation can be achieved, and it's through innovation that we bring new solutions to existing and past challenges. In Part 4, we look at innovation as a valuable outcome to collaboration, with the key being the method by which innovation is introduced, approached, and sustained. We will discuss successful and proven approaches to collaborative innovation by way of the most efficient means of influencing, assessing, testing, and introducing innovation without slowing the momentum of operational effectiveness.

PART 4

Capturing and Capitalizing on Innovation

Although it's been said by many different people in many different ways, there really is nothing new under the sun. In fact the statement I've heard the most when working with organizations and associations in introducing the ideas and practices we've discussed is "We've tried this before," most often followed up quickly by either ". . . and it didn't work" or ". . . and for some reason we stopped doing it." My response is always the same. Just because you tried something once and the results weren't as you expected, doesn't mean you should stop trying, or never approach it again. It simply means you go back to the drawing board. Obstacles and challenges when introducing any change are a sign of success.

This is where a robust approach to introducing collaborative innovation can yield significant results in creating more empowered and effective operations. New ideas are the very life blood of improvement, without which you would be hard pressed to find a solution that gains the buy-in of everyone involved.

In Part 4, I'll discuss what collaborative innovation is, and how you can create it, capitalize on it, and use it to improve operational effectiveness. The key, however, is not so much in how you approach collaborative innovation, but in whom you involve and engage with. Let's begin with Chapter 11 in which I will introduce you to my Operational Innovation model as the most effective means to breathe life and new opportunities into your organization.

10

Innovation Where You Least Expect It

Tapping into Unexpected Sources and Strategies

Although the origins of innovation date back to the 1500s, from a business perspective we seem to have become enamored with the concept. Despite the significant changes that have occurred as a result of the transition from the industrial age to the information age, organizationally the continued search for ways by which to improve operational effectiveness remains. The CEOs that I encounter are, for example, continually seeking ideas and opportunities to integrate technology in order to create new products and new services, and to provide new ways to offer value and connect with customers, clients, and members. Virtually anything that aligns with this desire tends to be referred to as innovation, however, it hinges heavily on the ability to collaborate. Unfortunately, this desire has yielded dozens, if not hundreds, of marketing firms offering to help make companies more "innovative" helping them stand out among their competitors.

I want to help us step back for a moment to consider what innovation truly is, how we can integrate and apply it, and the benefits we can expect to receive as a result. I am not trying to sell you on adopting innovation, but instead to clarify how every business, be it in the services, technology, healthcare, power generation, public sector, or manufacturing space, can capitalize on innovation, but only if first it embraces empowering employees, and second, if it operates within an environment of collaboration.

Let me start by suggesting that innovation is not simply a new method, idea, or product as defined by Wikipedia,[1] but more definitively it is the precise application of creativity yielding a different result. I want to point out a couple of distinctions in my definition. Innovation is not a process or approach, nor is it a definitive and beneficial outcome. Consider the following:

- Innovation requires that creativity be present.
- The value of creativity increases significantly when more people are involved.
- Creativity must yield an outcome.
- The outcome can be tangible or intangible.
- The outcome can be both positive and negative.

You may agree or disagree with my points above, but let me elaborate on a few of the most critical points. Business innovation is not valuable if there is no clear outcome. This is like making an investment in a research and development department that never yields a new product, service, or approach. It's a sunken investment with no return. Business innovation must have an outcome that presents an opportunity. Opportunities, however, are more likely to reach an outcome when a broader and more diverse group of people are involved. Innovation can result in an improvement to "how" something is done (such as a revised approach or process), or it can be a tangible product. Not every innovation results in the expected success, but this by no means is a reason to cease or avoid innovation. Ultimately the value of the outcome should not be limited to or measured against the investment. You can't put a price on creativity.

As I mentioned earlier, we are enamored, possibly even obsessed, with the idea that innovation must be present if we are to evolve our business in the pursuit of growth and profitability. In this chapter, I want to shift away from this discussion and focus more intently on the fact that innovation exists in every business, regardless of sector, and that the pursuit, integration, and outcomes of innovation require little more than a clear approach to achieving such, all of which is hinged upon your employees. Stated in a different way, you cannot achieve innovative outcomes if you are unwilling to engage with and empower your employees in support of innovation. The ability of a for-profit or not-for-profit business to achieve innovation is directly proportional to the degree to which employees believe in, support, and nurture innovation.

Do I have your attention? Let's first begin by talking about where you can find innovation inside your organization.

Innovation: Tapping into Rich Veins of New Ideas

Recently I did some work with an association, during which time we discussed how to tap into the intelligence of membership in order to increase member retention, referrals, and the value of programs and offerings. These areas also parallel in any for-profit organization simply by replacing "members" with "customers." The conduit to achieving these outcomes existed with the employees inside of the association, and I'm not referring just to the member-facing employees. During our discussions, we outlined the various touchpoints that each employee had with existing and new members, as well as their companies, colleagues, and even spouses. Figure 10.1 shows the Innovation Association Growth model that we used.

FIGURE 10.1 Innovation Association Growth Model

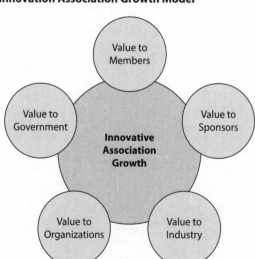

Through our discussions, we defined the touchpoints that each employee had with members, as well as their initial creative ideas on how they might further strengthen the value that members received from their interaction and the association, both today and in the future.

Here is a snapshot of a few of the areas that we uncovered innovative ideas within:

Touchpoint 1: Reception

Most often the first touchpoint with members when they called the association.

The ability to build a powerful first impression of the association; its willingness to serve the interests of members.

Innovative idea: Capture call-in names of members and send a follow-up touchpoint to ensure their needs were satisfied. Examples include a greeting card, follow-up e-mail, or voice message.

Touchpoint 2: Accounting

Interacts with members for renewal payments of membership fees and investment in offerings.

The ability to treat members like individuals with distinct needs rather than an account receivable; receive firsthand information on concerns with pricing, payment options, and competitiveness with other associations.

Innovative idea: Capture member questions and concerns relative to pricing, dues, and member offerings, and meet with the membership director and marketing once each month to review and discuss strategies.

Touchpoint 3: Events

Individuals responsible for events had the greatest number of personal interactions with members at events and conferences, as well as interactions with peers of other associations at networking events.

The ability not only to coordinate smooth-running, hiccup-free events, but to see virtually every member at an event, offering the opportunity to make a personal connection with the association as well as obtain intelligence relative to making the event more valuable to members.

Innovative idea: Interact with a minimum of 10 members for 10 minutes each at every event, asking distinct questions about what drew them to the event. What would make the event more valuable? What areas and topics are attractive for future events? Capture information and meet with marketing, sales, and membership relations following each event to discuss findings and generate ideas to improve future events.

Touchpoint 4: Corporate Affairs

As a department, corporate affairs had the greatest number of interactions with members of the association board at board meetings, committee meetings, and other events.

The ability to understand the gap between the perceptions that board members have of the value the association offers to members and the members' perception of the value the association provides.

Innovative idea: Create a monthly forum for individually and randomly selected members to interact one-on-one with board members to discuss the mission of the association and how it can provide further value to members. Capture the discussions for the board members to report at each board meeting to educate other members as to the changing needs, desires, and demographics of members.

Employees Offer a Conduit

Despite the example above referencing an association, the reality is that employees in any organization, be it a for-profit or not-for-profit, are the most connected as it pertains to providing value to customers, clients, or members. As we discussed briefly in Chapter 7, traditionally we have relied on sales and marketing to develop, build, and nurture relationships with customers, educating the rest of the organization on exactly what needs to happen in order to grow the business, but there are some fundamental flaws with this approach, specifically:

1. Salespeople are in a biased position as it pertains to providing information that is in the customers' or clients' best interest if it does not serve their own best interest.
2. Marketing is limited in scope (and creativity) by the budget constraints and historically accepted practices by which customers have been educated around product or service value.
3. There is often very little trust between sales and marketing, and the "balance" of most organizations as a result of the favoritism that is often perceived from being in a "making revenue" position versus a "spending revenue" position. (If you don't believe me, just ask the CFO or VP of finance as to the strength of his or her relationship with the VP of sales.)
4. In many instances, sales has a single touchpoint with the customer, whereas the balance of the business consists of multiple touchpoints (finance, shipping, quality control, production), creating differing perceptions on what the customer values and how the value should be delivered (which further exacerbates point 3 above).
5. Sales is often compensated for selling, so it is not often deemed a valuable use of a salesperson's time to educate employees in other areas on what the customer values and how the value can best be delivered.

For innovation to exist and be capitalized on, it's critical to identify and build connections with each and every employee because each one is capable of offering ideas, solutions, and suggestions that add value to your customer offerings. Innovation is not something that can or should be assigned to a specific department such as research and development, but an outcome that flourishes when employee ideas are enticed, attracted, tested, built, and appreciated. More on this later in the chapter.

How to Avoid Deflating Employee Innovation

The last point about building business innovation through employees is how to avoid common mistakes that deflate innovation. Building on the points above related to why sales and marketing are not the best sources of ideas for increasing value to customers, there are actions and approaches that often naturally occur in businesses today that result in a lack of employee-based innovation, many of which have been formed through our inverted approach to management and our desire for stringent processes and policies to govern consistency and productivity. The following principles and practices will help you avoid deflating employee innovation:

1. **Recognize all ideas as valuable ideas.** There are no bad ideas, just ideas with differing levels of value that require further dissemination in order to ascertain value.

2. **A visible idea is a valuable idea.** An idea that is not written down and displayed is an idea that never happened.

3. **Value ideas, don't vet them.** Eliminating ideas by committee is akin to telling employees who is smart and who is dumb. Identify business needs in advance, and evaluate ideas for priority, not elimination.

4. **Communicated idea value creates a value vortex.** The greater the knowledge that employees have of the impact of an idea, the greater the value of future ideas submitted by employees.

5. **Rewards reap rewards.** Recognition of ideas and their value goes a long way to enticing employees to submit further ideas. We all seek appreciation for the value of our inputs.

6. **Attraction is more enticing then demand.** Recognizing an idea that is put into action forms the belief that ideas are valued, creating the gravity required to attract further ideas.

7. **Novelty never wears off.** As business and customer needs evolve, so too will ideas that support the evolution. The novelty of presenting a creative solution never wears off when shifts in the business are clearly recognized.

8. **Ideas have no shelf life.** The integration of new ideas and solutions can take time, but this is no reason to eliminate ideas that have existed for some time.

To obtain the value of creative ideas from employees, the key is to avoid deflating the source of the ideas—most often the employees. With this in mind then, let's turn to discussing other sources of innovation that you can capitalize on for your business.

Five Sources of Innovation to Consider

Most of the popular folklore around innovation exists with businesses that have been able to capitalize on employee innovation as I described above. At the risk of overusing common examples, we've all heard of Apple's creative process, how Disney brings new ideas to fruition, and Sir Branson's quest to bring space travel to the masses. These are all relevant examples, but the sources of innovation extend well beyond employees and offer additional opportunities to build a competitive advantage and bridge employee ideas with other ideas. Put another way, in order to capitalize on these sources of innovation, it's critical to ensure that employees are engaged in the process.

At a macro level, innovation exists both internally (as described above) and externally. So far we've discussed at length employee innovation that is internal to every organization, so now I want to turn our focus on the sources of external innovation, of which there are most commonly five across all sectors and industries (Figure 10.2), namely:

1. Suppliers or contractors
2. Customers
3. Competitors
4. Peers
5. Industry

Each of these sources of innovation offers an opportunity to increase the volume, relevance, and value of ideas and solutions to build more

FIGURE 10.2 External Sources of Innovation

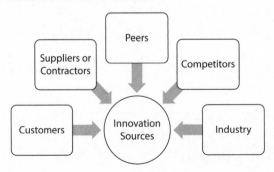

enticing products, cutting-edge services, and unique offerings that help a business stand out in the marketplace. The key is that the internal innovators, the employees that work within a business, must be empowered to achieve any valuable or measurable innovation with and through these sources.

External Innovation: Suppliers and Contractors

Most businesses rely on a series of supporting suppliers or contractors. Even the smallest business, such as a hair salon, coffee shop, or automotive dealer, requires interaction and partnership with a series of suppliers, not the least of which can include:

- A corporate franchise office
- Suppliers of tools or equipment for the business
- Service providers to maintain equipment and tools
- Advertising agencies and media
- Marketing firms
- Employee development and training providers (online and in person)
- Landlords or lease owners
- Property management

What's critical about all of these relationships is that within each there often exists a more complete knowledge about the specific product or service than what the business's owner or employees know, and not tapping into this information is a clear way to avoid new ideas and solutions that would help the business extend itself beyond its competitors.

While helping organizations create more value focused supply chains, I've noticed a disturbing trend that is hindering innovation. Those in external facing roles such as contract management, sourcing, and procurement have been educated and trained to avoid innovation, not entice it. I've taken polls with CEOs in the various forums that I speak at and found almost unanimously that their external facing employees are often not trained in or incentivized to entice and pursue external innovation. External facing activities, (for example, those with suppliers and contractors) are most often measured as successful based on how quickly and effectively a solution can be introduced. Time for collaboration and creativity is not encouraged or possible in these aggressive timelines. In fact, I've found through my work with organizations globally that there are several habits that hinder an organization's ability to tap into external innovation, namely:

- There is no mechanism for new suppliers or external partners to identify or demonstrate their unique product or service offerings.
- Employees desire to avoid distractions in order to be "productive" often results in unreturned phone calls and ignored e-mail messages from external sources of new products and services.
- Existing needs of the business are often unclear and undefined relative to those internally that interact with external suppliers, contractors, and affiliates.
- Existing suppliers are managed closely and under strict policy and scrutiny, and are not encouraged to submit new ideas, and so believe their business is at risk if they venture beyond what is considered "normal business."
- There is no enticement for new or existing suppliers to offer new solutions (i.e., there is no reward for this).
- There is no facilitated means of allowing suppliers to collaborate and identify new innovative solutions.

To resolve these limitations to supplier innovation, I help clients introduce several changes that ultimately resulted in greater collaboration with both new and existing suppliers and more innovative ideas that supported both the business and its customers. Some examples of these solutions included:

1. Introducing supplier innovation forums where several business challenges are presented to noncompeting suppliers, following which facilitated discussions occur between these groups and internal employees to identify new solutions and ideas to overcome the challenges.

2. Educating employees on the importance of meeting with external parties, such as suppliers and contractors, and the value the interaction could bring, particularly with their understanding of business needs.
3. Introducing expectations and measures around meeting with new and existing suppliers, contractors, and peers on a monthly basis with the sole expectation of identifying new products, services, or solutions that would support business needs, objectives, and vision.
4. Introducing rewards for those suppliers, contractors, or affiliates that collaborated with a company on new and innovative solutions or products that in turn yielded better results for the business, its customers, and the supplier.

I've introduced other, more subtle changes as well, but you get the picture. In order to capitalize on relationships with suppliers and contractors, it's important to introduce and sustain the following:

1. Ensure that external partners are aware of your business challenges and opportunities.
2. Create a forum for introduction and discussion of these challenges and opportunities on a regular basis.
3. Entice or attract feedback from new external partners by being open to inquiries and requests for meetings.
4. Collaborate with external partners in the introduction of new ideas and opportunities.
5. Shoot for mutual successes in the introduction of new ideas and opportunities—make it a win-win.
6. Share in the rewards of new ideas and opportunities. Further ideas come from shared successes.

External Innovation: Customers

There is no doubt that interacting with customers is key to building a stronger and more profitable business. As we've discussed multiple times in this book, it's simply not enough to sell a quality product or deliver a fantastic service to a customer in today's globally competitive economy and expect to solidify long-term sustainable customer relationships. This is where customer innovation adds the greatest value. By collaborating with customers to bring new and innovative solutions to life, the relationship and reliance on the relationship becomes deeply engrained.

We are surrounded by sources of customer innovation that are easily recognizable. Dropbox, reported as being one of the most innovative companies of 2014,[2] is one such example. Dropbox continues to interact with both consumers and businesses in order to expand the user-ability of the solution across multiple platforms. As new devices are introduced to the marketplace, Dropbox works to ensure that its solution interacts easily and seamlessly, making its product a no-brainer for customers. Dropbox has also placed additional energy into collaborating not just with consumers but also with business users by adding project-management features for workplace users.

A close friend of mine, Shawn Ringel, is the general manager of a Nissan dealership. In such a highly competitive and price-sensitive market, Shawn participates in numerous sources of innovation to ensure that his dealership and team continuously raise the bar to provide outstanding products and service to existing and potential customers. Some examples of collaborative innovation that Shawn participates in include:

1. Monthly meetings with Nissan in face-to-face "rap" sessions to discuss ideas and provide feedback on products, services, pricing, features, and competitive opportunities.
2. Shawn also participates in a dealer advisory board, a subset of dealers who interact with Nissan designers and engineers helping to ensure model revisions and future models meet the demands and desires of customers.
3. Shawn and his team of managers in sales and service participate in a series of portals in order to remain current on product and service updates from Nissan; to remain current on training in using, installing, and repairing new products, and to obtain and exchange information on customer incentive programs.

4. Shawn also holds daily meetings with his team to ensure that he facilitates connections between customer feedback and Nissan. These meetings allow him to keep his team up to date on any changes in products or services, as well as to ensure that customer concerns are understood and engage all stakeholders from the Nissan factory right down to his technicians.

The most successful customer innovations then are built upon several key elements:

1. A definitive description and demonstration of the value to customers resulting from the collaboration.
2. Consistent interactions with customers to prompt innovative discussions and sharing of challenges and ideas, both formally and informally.
3. Clarity surrounding business needs and objectives contrasted against customer needs and objectives to link the most opportune instances for collaboration and innovation.
4. The willingness to provide the lion's share of rewards to the customers, with the indirect value of sustaining a stronger and more stable customer relationship going to the supplier or contractor.
5. The ability to extend ideas and solutions beyond a single customer relationship, allowing for sharing of the innovation across a broader band of customers.
6. Promotion of ideas and outcomes to other customers to entice engagement and interaction.

Customer innovation is not only a valuable interaction for building new products and solutions that can be used elsewhere in the marketplace, it also brings insight into new products and services that customers actually need.

External Innovation: Competitors

Uber, the app that connects consumers requiring transportation with a crowd of drivers, was first founded as UberCab by Travis Kalanick and

Garrett Camp in 2009. The app (the key component to Uber's growth) was later released in June 2010.[3] The app that accompanied Uber was the key differentiator in the market, allowing Uber a competitive advantage until new, low-cost crowd sourcing competition such as Lyft, Sidecar, and Haxi began to emerge. Uber has added additional services to compete with these lower cost providers, including UberTaxi (partnerships with local taxi services), and UberX (nonluxury vehicles). In addition to warding off competition, Uber continues to innovate by testing courier services such as UberRush in Manhattan and UberPool (car-pooling and ride-sharing programs) in San Francisco. What Uber is doing is continuously innovating to adjust and improve its existing model by considering both its direct and indirect competition.

Competitor innovation results from five steps, namely:

1. Completion of a Product Service Competitive Analysis (Figure 10.3) to identify existing and future competitive opportunities. This approach requires the business to consider all of the components of its existing offerings in contrast to consumer and business needs in the market.
2. A frequent and thorough review of the marketplace against the most appealing products and services based on the breakdown. This includes formation of creative ideas for improvement of existing products or services to capture new market opportunities, or creation of new products or services to achieve the same. The starting point should always be improvement, as costs associated with introducing a revised but existing product into a new market are considerably less than building or creating a new product or service.
3. Identification of costs and revenue as it compares to the product service breakdown to ascertain priorities relative to research and development of new competitive products.
4. Research and development of new or modified products or services that rival competitors' products or services based on steps 1 through 3 above.
5. Testing, validation, and introduction of new solutions to the marketplace.

FIGURE 10.3 Competitive Innovation Assessment

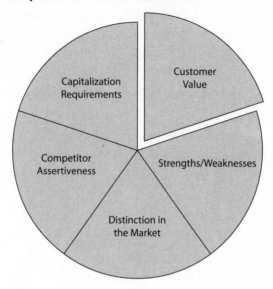

Competitive innovation is derived from the ability to identify and remain current on all direct and indirect competitive offerings in order to identify new market opportunities to pursue or improvements that should be made to existing products and services.

External Innovation: Peers

Groups like Vistage, TEC, and YPO offer CEOs and executives the opportunity to learn from their peers. As a frequent speaker in these forums, the feedback I receive from members is that there is much that can be learned from peers in other industries and sectors. This is the value in peer innovation. Belonging to a group with colleagues and peers from other industries allows for the consideration of new and unique ideas that may support a competitive advantage.

Peer innovation may seem unrealistic, but consider that drive-through windows, now commonplace at many banks, were introduced as a result of their popularity at restaurants. Hundreds of manufacturing companies and associations are incorporating online chat features into their websites due to the success telecom companies have had in using these tools to engage with existing and potential customers. There are a myriad of ideas in business today that are the result of peer innovation.

Many of my clients who belong to the executive forums I mentioned apply the following steps to introduce peer innovation:

1. Invest time in networking and interacting with peers from different industries.
2. Share and discuss challenges and opportunities that exist in contrasting businesses, being open to ideas that others have applied for similar challenges despite differences in business models, customer base, or geography.
3. Form ideation grounds where ideas are collected and are further considered and improved upon by business resource groups including executives, managers, and employees.
4. Welcome ideas from outside resources such as consultants and contractors, who bring knowledge and experience from different industries and sectors.
5. Test new ideas with a subset of your market to identify interest, uptake, and additional improvement opportunities.

External Innovation: Industry

The last form of innovation that I want to discuss is industry innovation. This is innovation that is not captured from competitors or peers, but new ideas and solutions that emerge within your industry that can be further considered to improve the value of your existing products and services.

Blockbuster's failure as a company is a good example of how ignoring industry innovation can kill a company. As the video industry began to shift toward online offerings such as Netflix, Blockbuster was faced with the challenge of quickly converting its brick-and-mortar operation to a virtual operation, a shift that Blockbuster failed to pursue fast enough to keep pace with changing consumer demands. The end result was bankruptcy, as customers flocked to rent movies online rather than in a store.

Being aware of and taking rapid action toward introducing innovations that exists across your industry is another means of staying relevant and revenue strong. The steps to industry innovation that I assist clients with introducing are as follows:

1. Remain current on industry shifts through participation in forums, events, online media, and research.
2. Continuously review emerging shifts within the industry relative to your existing model considering the following three questions:
   - How would this shift offer additional or renewed value to our existing or new customers?
   - What would be the most relevant and risk-adverse area within our business to test this approach?
   - How quickly can we move to test this innovation in order to determine its scope and relevance to improving our market position?
3. Ensure existing business processes facilitate rapid introduction of new ideas into existing and new markets.

After considering the five sources of innovation above, I want to bring a few key points to your attention that can make or break your intent to introduce and reap value from an investment in innovation, namely:

1. **Innovation is not singular.** It's impossible to introduce, sustain, or obtain value from innovation if the responsibility for innovation is placed in the hands of one person or a single department.
2. **Innovation requires awareness.** If employees are unaware of the business challenges and opportunities that exist, there is little chance that they will present ideas to support overcoming the challenges or pursuing the opportunities.
3. **Innovation requires empowerment.** New ideas will not arise if employees are not empowered to take action toward the identification, consideration, and integration of innovative solutions and ideas.

4. **Innovation is built on recognition.** If you suggest to employees that their ideas aren't valuable, the number and frequency of ideas will continue to wane. The more you appreciate the value of employee ideas, the more ideas you will have to appreciate.

5. **The best ideas don't happen naturally.** Innovation requires an open and facilitated approach to interacting with employees from:
   - Your existing industry
   - Other outside industries
   - Competitors
   - Customers
   - Peers

It's virtually impossible to obtain consistent and meaningful value from innovation if lines of communication don't exist or are hindered between employees at all levels of a business and those within the areas identified above.

I've mentioned earlier in this book that employees offer your greatest source of competitive advantage. Innovation is *the* mechanism that directly supports achieving this advantage. By pursuing each of the various sources of innovation in the manner described above, you will find a plethora of new and creative solutions to ensure the long-term profitability and viability of your business.

Innovation: Creating Ideas with Impact

We've talked extensively about the value of innovation, how to ensure a valuable pipeline of innovative ideas, and the various sources from within which you can capture innovation. With all of this information in mind, the obvious question becomes how to bring to life all of these ideas that are floating around.

As with anything else, capitalizing on innovation requires a process. Just because a company wants to be or talks of being innovative, doesn't mean it is (despite what its marketing and promotions may suggest to you—Kodak once considered itself highly innovative, yet its inability to capitalize rapidly on the most valuable ideas resulted in the demise of the business).

Many ideas exist relative to how innovation can or should be introduced into a business or association. I want to introduce you to the process that I have helped clients apply in order to ensure that the best ideas are brought forward and acted on.

For ideas to be brought to life, there must be processes in place to facilitate this, namely:

1. **Opportunities to create new ideas.** Considering each of the key sources of innovation identified above, what opportunities exist to identify new ideas? Are ideation sessions offered that allow employees an opportunity to delineate and create possible solutions for company challenges? It's not uncommon to observe a board of directors brainstorming ideas to overcome association or business challenges. Ideas are shared among a group of peers with different backgrounds and experience, and then once defined they are voted on relative to actions to be taken. It is rare to see a similar approach between employees and suppliers or employees and management, but this is the necessary component to ensure bringing forth the most creative and valuable ideas.

2. **Opportunities to further improve existing ideas.** Lean rapid improvement events, as an example, involve a component in which the participants spend time idealizing how to improve the value of process steps while eliminating waste. There are no boundaries or barriers to their ideas, and everyone is encouraged to share. To obtain fresh ideas, steps are necessary to allow ideation and creativity to occur. Innovation is more than new ideas; it is the ability to bring improvements to life. The iPod is a result of product innovation, derived from the concept of a Walkman with the integration of digital music in a smaller and easy-to-carry package.

3. **Test ideas for relevance and value.** As we discussed in Chapter 4, I've long been a proponent of including input from employees in the formulation of a business strategy. In addition, I've often incorporated scenario planning where individuals participating in the strategy session are split into groups to further test and validate ideas

to ascertain if their pursuit is valuable considering the future vision of the organization. This is a great example of how to test ideas for their relevance and value, and a method that I have helped clients introduce as part of their innovation journey. Ensuring a cross section of employees have the chance to consider, test, and trial ideas is key to ensuring the ideas that are pursued are those that are most relevant and present the greatest value.

4. **Introduction of ideas to reap value.** It was once said that an idea that is never introduced is just an idea. With the most valuable ideas prioritized, tested, and validated, the next logical step is to put the ideas into action. Dependent on the perceived impact of the idea, this may be best done through a trial or pilot, or it may require a full-blown large-scale implementation. (I've never been a proponent of pilots if the implementation is planned for a larger scale, as it tends to result in less preparation and lower value produced through the pilot than if it were considered and planned as the large implementation it was intended to be.) Developing processes and plans for introduction of ideas is the key step to reaping the rewards of the investment of time and energy spent.

5. **Recognition of those who supported the process.** My client Larsen and Shaw has an *idea board* where ideas are captured from employees, reviewed by a random subset of employees on a regular basis, and then put into action. Past ideas that have been introduced are kept visual in an attempt to demonstrate appreciation of employee ideas, as well as to prompt further thinking. It's not uncommon during my visits to see at least one employee reviewing the board, having new ideas that they are looking to further vet against past ideas and initiatives. Ideas that are rewarded are ideas that get repeated. Finding a simple means to identify the progress of ideas and to reward and recognize those that participated in the process is critical to ensuring that the influx of creative solutions remains consistent.

From our discussions on innovation, you may have noticed some underlying components to success, specifically the ability to collaborate internally and externally, as well as the empowerment of employees to become engaged in and take action toward innovation. In Chapter 11, I want to continue our discussion of innovation and dive deeper into exactly how to extract value from your innovation efforts in order to reap significant and measurable rewards.

11

The Innovation Approach
From Conception to Outcome

I n Chapter 10, we spent time discussing what innovation is and isn't; we also discussed the internal and external sources of innovation and key ideas on how to capitalize on innovation. With the sources of innovation identified, the next logical step is to consider introducing a process to facilitate innovation. As we discussed in the last chapter, creative and valuable ideas exist both internally and externally to a business. However, without placing a focused effort on how to prompt, attract, and entice these ideas in order to bring them to reality, they will cease to emerge.

Equally important is that once the ideas are presented, there must be a proven method by which they are captured, categorized, prioritized, piloted, and introduced. As I mentioned earlier, an idea that is not capitalized upon is an idea that has no legs. If you were to begin to tap into and collaborate with the various sources of creative ideas and solutions that surround your business today, you would quickly face the overwhelming task of determining which idea to pursue first.

We will also discuss the fact that innovation is not a singular process, but a complementary means to improve business performance and increase the value of outcomes, engaging various internal and external sources in a manner that shifts away from the traditionally favored approach to harboring business intelligence as a secret weapon. I will introduce the Innovation Model, a six-step process to introducing innovation into any business, be it in manufacturing, distribution, or service-based, for-profit or not-for-profit.

Lastly, I will draw a distinction between a company's ability to collaborate both internally and externally, and its ability to introduce innovation that adds value, which is the very reason why we discussed collaboration earlier in Part 3. Innovation will not serve as a valuable tool for increasing business performance and success if there is little willingness or ability to collaborate both internally within the business and externally with suppliers, customers, peers, and industry.

I recognize that some of you may have turned to this chapter first as a result of your desire to introduce innovation into your organization, so let's begin by discussing how to set priorities along your innovation journey.

Innovation Requires Facilitation: Ideas with Impact

Several years ago I was working with an energy firm that had introduced what it considered a means to identify and capitalize on innovative ideas within the hearts and minds of its employees. The firm intended to facilitate the process through an employee suggestion program. The program was introduced as a method to ensure that all employees had the opportunity to suggest ideas that they felt would help the company reduce costs and increase efficiencies. Indirectly, it was also deemed by the executive team as a great means to facilitate the uncovering of employee concerns and frustrations in order to identify where time and money should be invested to help improve the culture of the business. (Note that this company did not yet understand that its efforts for improving culture would have been better invested in building community—see Chapter 5, "Engage the Masses: Building a Continuous Improvement Community.")

With various forms, processes, and a centralized e-mail database set up to facilitate the inbound ideas, staff were *temporarily dedicated* to the role of reviewing, mining, and responding to the inbound employee suggestions (their perception was that the inbound ideas would only last for a brief period of time), and the program was launched. At the heart of the program was the desire to have the temporary staff accept and filter all inbound communications, forwarding an agenda to a small panel of employees and managers for review and selection, with final approval residing with the executive sponsor. The entire process was expected to be complete within a two-week period; hence employees were advised of an expected turnaround response of 14 days for all inbound inquiries made.

Within two weeks of the launch of the program, the new administrators were overwhelmed with both handwritten suggestions submitted by employees in the strategically placed "suggestion boxes" and hundreds of inbound e-mail questions, concerns, and complaints. No sooner had the program been launched than it was quickly spiraling out of control; response times to employee feedback quickly reached 30 to 45 days. As the program moved into its fourth week, the backlog of suggestions had grown to 60 days. Employees began to voice concerns about response times and lack of a priority to their requests. In an effort to reduce response time, the processes for screening, review, approval, and introduction were expedited, resulting in more stringent filters at the initial response level (more ideas were rejected upon response thereby reducing the number of ideas that were presented to the panel for review). The increased filtering by frontline staff meant that employees were receiving a more rapid response to their suggestions, but the responses were from unqualified and not typically knowledgeable employees who weren't able to properly justify their decisions.

Despite the continued addition of new resources to the employee suggestion review team, the program continued to falter as initiatives requested by the panel turned into larger scale projects for which there was no funding and few resources to support.

I share this example with you because it is exactly how *not* to initiate innovation.

I meet hundreds of CEOs through executive forums such as Vistage and TEC, as well as at various venues and association events. When I ask how they are incorporating innovation into their business, the response I receive is almost always tied to a belief that innovation is captured in an existing employee suggestion program that they believe draws upon and supports the introduction of creative ideas, or through a continuous improvement program that entices and introduces creative ideas through collaboration in order to overcome bottlenecks and obstructions in business performance. Neither of these is a true innovation model, although they are tools and approaches that can be incorporated into innovation to facilitate the process itself.

As we've already discussed extensively, the value of innovation, how to ensure a valuable pipeline of innovative ideas, and the various sources from which you can capture innovation, the obvious question that remains is how exactly to bring all of these new ideas to life, doing so with minimal time, effort, and investment. This is a logical question for which there is a logical answer—or there should be if you've paid attention to our discussions in earlier chapters of this book. Let me explain.

As with anything else, capitalizing on innovation requires a process. As I mentioned in Chapter 10, just because a company wants to be or speaks of being innovative doesn't mean it is.

Building a Foundation for Innovation

There are a plethora of opinions relative to how innovation should be introduced into an organization. The reality is that innovation cannot and will not exist in its most valuable and desirable form if groundwork isn't first laid for its existence. This is step one before ever considering a model for integrating innovation (an example of which I will introduce to you in a moment), but first we need to consider the aspects of an effective foundation to ensure that innovation is sustainable:

1. **Executive-employee connection.** Do your executives engage with and support your employees? For innovation to exist there first must be a clear alignment and connection between what executives *and* employees believe the priorities of the business to be. In Chapter 3 we discussed the employee disconnect. As innovation is built upon collaboration, there must be a clear connection between executives and employees.

2. **Strategic strings.** As innovation relies on the most valuable and powerful ideas being brought to the forefront and acted upon, it's crucial that employees first understand, support, and connect their role with the vision of the company. If strategic strings for employees are missing, it's likely that there will be a lack of agreement and visibility on which ideas are the most relevant and powerful relative to where the business is attempting to go.

3. **A community of improvement.** Innovation is not simply about generating ideas. An idea is only as valuable as the outcome it produces. For this reason, it's critical that employees embrace new ideas and change, which is the underlying tenet of a community of improvement. Ideas that are brought forth must add value to the business, its customers, and especially its employees if the employees involved are going to embrace and act upon the changes necessary to bring the idea to life. This is at the forefront of the community of improvement that we discussed in Chapter 5.

4. **Value connection.** For employees to embrace the introduction of the most valuable innovations there must first be a clear connection with the customers, what they value, and how it can be best facilitated. This is an individual connection each employee must make with the business's customers if they are to take the right actions to support adding steadily increasing value to both existing and prospective customers of the business.

5. **Collaboration conglomeration.** Through incorporation of the aforementioned four areas, a strong connection is built for each and every employee, executive, supplier, and customer relative to the desired future state of the organization. With clear understanding and relevance of the organization's desired direction, there must be a willingness and means set forth to facilitate collaboration. Collaboration is *the key* to ensuring that innovative opportunities are transparent, relevant, valuable, and attainable.

Do these critical aspects of an innovation foundation sound familiar? They should.

When you consider what must be present in an organization before innovation can exist, it brings to light exactly why I have chosen to speak of innovation at this point in the book, rather than earlier on. (Note: If you've jumped to this chapter first, I highly encourage you to spend some time reviewing the earlier chapters, as without building a proper foundation upon which innovation can exist and survive, it's highly unlikely that your innovation efforts will yield the results you expect or desire.)

Without a clear connection built between employees and:

- The objectives of senior management and the board
- The desired future state of the business
- That which customers value
- The opportunities internally and externally to breathe new life into the business

through innovation, all supported through a collective desire to improve the organizational performance and to increase value to customers, there is little chance that ideas will be innovative at all, much less supported and seen through to fruition.

The Empowered Innovation Model

Now that we've discussed the various components of innovation, I want to share with you my Empowered Innovation model as a means to facilitate the process of shifting from the concept of innovation toward putting innovative ideas into practice. In Figure 11.1 you will notice that there are six distinct phases to the model, many of which we have discussed earlier in this chapter.

Source Selection

The first phase of innovation is to consider the sources that exist and are relevant based on your business objectives. It's illogical to decide to pursue internal and external innovation all at once, and it

FIGURE 11.1 Empowered Innovation Model

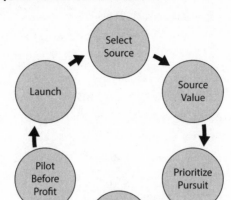

does not make sense to simply note internal innovation as a starting point. As a clear starting point (and road map to success along your innovation journey), consider the areas of the business that would be the ideal starting point for collaboration by considering the following questions:

1. Where would innovation have the greatest impact on our business today? Consider new products, new services, improved processes, and improvement to existing products or services as a starting point.
2. For each area of impact, list the possible sources of innovation, starting with considering whether sources are internal, external, or both.
3. Beginning with internal innovation, which departments are best positioned or suited to participate in the areas of internal innovation you have identified? This should extend to include other divisions of the business, board members, and internal contractors.

4. Where you've noted external innovation as sources, identify which customers, suppliers, contractors, consultants, or other external resources are best positioned to add value to the process. You want to note any and all relevant sources for each innovative need (products, services, processes, etc.).

5. Relative to the innovation sources map that you've now identified, what gaps might exist today? Are there specific groups, departments, customers, or other resources that are not addressed—referring back again to point 1 above? Are there any existing knowledge gaps, experience gaps, intelligence gaps, market awareness gaps, new technology gaps, and so on?

6. Consider the future state. Where will your business be five or even ten years from today? Are there any additional sources (internal or external) that need to be added to your source map? What other gaps may exist between business needs today and in the future?

For a worksheet to identify your internal and external resources of innovation, as well as dozens of other resources to support empowering your business, visit www.operationalempowerment.com.

Source Value

For every source of innovation you have identified, it's critical to now ascertain what value it brings to the table. By working through this exercise, it will become readily apparent as to which sources might truly add value and which do not. During my time working in the energy sector, we were forced most often due to regulations to purchase products and services at prices well above market value. This isn't to say that the companies selling the products and services weren't adding value, but instead policies and regulations set forth by those outside of the business had a significant influence over how much money was spent. Considerable effort was often spent negotiating with suppliers to reduce pricing, when the greater value would be achieved by connecting and collaborating with the regulator to ensure that policies and regulations didn't impede the profitability (and ultimately the sustainability) of the business.

You might be wondering why so much effort is required to introduce innovation. The approach I use with my clients, and am sharing with you, is not meant as a rapid innovation approach but an innovation strategy. By investing the time early on in the innovation journey and identifying all of the various innovation sources and their value, you have information that will support sustainable and valuable innovation efforts. I view innovation as a continuum, so once the processes to capitalize on the sources are in place, the challenge becomes the continuation of further opportunities and sources for innovation. Luckily, by following my model this won't be a concern for you.

Prioritizing Pursuit

Once you begin this exercise as I've laid out, you will likely find that a plethora of information has been generated by this point, and that's good. Innovation is about ideas, and by identifying and tapping into various sources we strategically increase the value and robustness of the ideas that are generated and pursued, which is why step three is to prioritize your pursuit. Innovation, like other programs that support introducing organizational change, should begin with success in mind. Don't try to tackle everything, but instead pursue only a few ideas that have the greatest chance for positive impact in order to build momentum and support. This is not a time to reconstruct your entire business, but to find wins that further engage internal and external sources in supporting your innovation journey. Simply put, not every source of innovation is the best source, or the best place to start.

Relative to prioritizing innovation, I help my clients use a phased approach that begins with internal sources and shifts to external sources. To begin, select the opportunities for innovation that you believe will be the most successful, the most powerful, and have the greatest impact on your business. I would suggest starting with no fewer than five ideas, and no more than ten.

Then for each source consider the following questions and make note of your answers. This is often something that I help my clients do as it is best done in a collaborative fashion. You can achieve this by placing several of your most engaged and enthusiastic employees, managers, and executives in a room to collaborate on answers.

1. What is the value innovation may offer relative to each product, service, or process you've identified? What do you expect might be possible to achieve, and how will this help the business, its employees, customers, and the community?
2. What is the degree of difficulty (consider cost, time, resources) to pursuing innovation in this area? Remember that you want to begin with those innovation initiatives that offer the greatest potential value and best opportunity for success.
3. What is a realistic timeline to achieving these ideas? If you were to begin any of these initiatives today, how long might it be before you have some realistic and tangible outcomes?

As I've mentioned earlier, I'm a proponent of beginning with internal innovation opportunities before ever shifting to external innovation opportunities, and for good reason. To engage external sources can be a challenge if you don't have successes to point to. More specifically, consider:

- Would your customers be open to collaborating with you on innovation if you can't definitively speak to a proven process that you have incorporated to demonstrate valuable outcomes?
- Would suppliers engage in an innovative forum or project with your business, setting aside the possibility of future business (meaning the supplier would send individuals to participate who were not directly involved in sales or business development) if they were unable to witness some outcomes you've already experienced through your innovation process?
- Would a government agency support your innovative efforts if you were unable to demonstrate how your process has brought value to all participants involved (your company, customers, suppliers, your local region, etc.)?

The answer is clearly no. In order to engage external sources of innovation and obtain the greatest value and engagement from their participation, it's critical that you first have a proven process and outcomes that you can point to and use in your pitch to join your innovation crusade.

Preparing Your Approach

Every innovation opportunity can be distinct, which means that there is not necessarily a clear approach to pursue innovation that can be applied for every single situation. Predominantly the most unique differences are between internal and external innovation. In formulating the best approach to any type of innovation, however, it's critical to consider the five points mentioned in Chapter 10, namely:

1. Opportunities to create *new* ideas
2. Opportunities to further improve *existing* ideas
3. Testing of ideas for relevance and value
4. Introduction of ideas to reap value
5. Recognition of those who supported the process

Pilot Before Profit

I've repeatedly found that there are predominantly two schools of thought when it comes to initiating improvements and changes in business. I call this the "think versus act" mentality. There are those who prefer to wait, analyze, assess, obsess, and test ideas to death in order to prove them out before they are ever brought to life. This is the "think" approach. There is also the "act" mentality, which is the "get 'er done" method of business. There is no time to think about anything except checking another priority or task off the list. Of course success in any regard requires action, but there is a distinct balance between thinking (delaying introduction of new ideas) and acting (running toward shiny bright objects). By applying the approach in my Empowered Innovation model, you will notice there is a structure that forces some thought relative to preparation for pursuit of innovation, but following this, all steps focus on action. The model is constructed this way for a reason. With proper preparation and investment of time, there is little to worry about as it pertains to potential risks or gaps in the introduction and execution stages.

This is why step five is the "pilot" phase. It's during this phase that each change resulting from the innovation process enters into a pilot phase in order to assess its functionality, capability, and value. In some instances the simplicity of the innovation may not warrant a pilot, but in most instances I find that a pilot of a new idea is exactly what is required to move the innovation forward as quickly as possible. You've likely heard the story of how Post-it Notes were first created through an accidental discovery of an incredibly weak adhesive by Spencer Silver while working for 3M. Despite the desire to find a home for the reusable adhesive, it wasn't until another employee, Art Fry, came up with the idea of using the adhesive to keep his song page markers intact in his hymn book at church that the idea came to fruition. This was the first official pilot of the adhesive, and although successful, it was found to delaminate paper when removed from the page. This feedback was then turned over to two additional 3M employees, Roger Merrill and Henry Courtney, who developed a coating that could be applied to the back of paper to make sure the adhesive stuck to the paper and didn't delaminate when peeled away from other surfaces. The result was the introduction of sticky notes to the commercial market in 1977 (some nine years after the inception of the accidental adhesive).[1] It was through innovation that this accidental adhesive was converted to a multimillion-dollar idea used around the world today. In the instance of Post-it Notes, piloting and testing that was initially considered a waste of time and money, lead to the opportunity to create a saleable product.

The key for any pilot then is to ensure that robust mechanisms are in place during the pilot to collect and feed any relevant information (positive or not) into a forum in which it can be captured, analyzed by the original innovation forum, and included as a component to formulating an improved innovation.

Launching Innovation

Ideas are only as valuable as their outcomes. With ideas piloted and proven, the final stage in the innovation model is to bring the idea to life in real time. No different from introducing changes to existing products, services, or processes, launching innovative ideas requires a separate process to bring the ideas to life.

There are five steps to realizing valuable outcomes from innovation efforts:

1. **Introduction of the idea.** Like any effective change, it's important to introduce innovative ideas, changes, and improvements to those it will impact, or who will participate in its execution. Obtaining commitment and engagement in the innovation early on is a matter of answering the critical question, "What's in it for them?" By introducing the idea in advance of its official introduction, you ward off concerns or obstacles that may later serve as a detriment to your innovation.

2. **Training, education, and marketing.** You might be thinking that training and education are predominantly used in process innovations, whereas education and marketing are typically part of product or service innovation. Not so. When introducing changes internally or externally, you must be prepared to educate on the particulars of the innovation, train those involved in using or pursuing the innovation, and market, market, market. Even if the innovation is not for sale, you still have to market its value in order to obtain buy-in and support (refer to point 1 above).

3. **Managing the paper trail.** Are there business processes, new product introductions, warranties, media, or any other information that must be updated in order to ensure that the innovation is solidified and considered a normal part of daily life?

4. **Reinforcement of expectations.** Even with pilots it's often difficult to mimic the real world. For this very reason it's important to ensure that everyone (both internally and externally) understands clearly in advance what the innovation is expected to do. It's through this education that any new value, limitations, or faults are quickly realized and addressed to ensure a sustained journey.

5. **Review and revisit.** Innovation is never finished. Reflecting on the example of 3M Post-it Notes, there have been continued innovations to the product throughout its life cycle that have included improved adhesion characteristics and new colors. Innovation needs to be periodically revisited by those most intimate with its intended value. Consider the simple question, Is this doing what it was intended to do? If not, what's changed or different? If it is, are we extracting additional value that we hadn't considered?

Procter & Gamble have long been recognized for its new product innovation. The business itself was built upon an innovative collaboration between William Procter and James Gamble, who achieved their initial business success by selling a soap that could be produced and sold for significantly less money than imported soaps.[2] Today P&G is dedicated to partnering with external sources such as inventors, engineers, and entrepreneurs through its "Connect + Learn" platform. P&G collaborates with external sources to develop, test, and introduce new products to the marketplace on a regular basis. P&G has also created a Co-Creation crowdsourcing platform allowing a broad interaction with external inventors, entrepreneurs, customers, and suppliers to develop and test new product innovations that might otherwise never see the marketplace. P&G's refined models, market relationships, and production capabilities allow it to select and introduce products to the market faster and more effectively than a smaller company might ever be able to achieve.

So far we've spent the predominance of this book discussing how to build a more empowered operation through collaboration and innovation that engage sources that exist both internally and externally to your organization. If your thoughts thus far are that these are great ideas that you may someday consider introducing, let me suggest to you that the future is now.

With the continued expansion of global competition, increasing competition for talent, and an insatiable consumer desire for personalization and customization, there is no better time to employ these concepts and ideas to build a stronger, more efficient operation.

Time is truly of the essence. Therefore it is imperative that not only do you introduce changes to how your organization operates, you must do it immediately. Don't believe me? Just look at some of the longest standing and most powerful companies of our time, companies that had cash and market share to spare, but who failed build a more empowered operation. Kodak, Blockbuster, American Suzuki Motor Company, and Groupon are all examples of companies that failed to build a more empowered operation to satisfy the shifts in customer demands and growing competition.

In Chapter 12, I want to address the last and most important point of this book: how to transition from the ideas and concepts discussed into powerful and pragmatic actions in order to affect significant and effective shifts in your operation. So grab a paper and pen and strap in—we are about to shift into high gear.

12

Empowerment Imperative

Transitioning from Thinking to Doing

Despite the best of intentions, there are numerous challenges that any business attempting to become more operationally empowered will face. This book is intended to identify the primary focus areas in which empowerment can be deeply integrated, allowing for the increased operational effectiveness of the organization and increased value for its customers, while generating increased passion, commitment, and creativity from employees to create a competitive advantage.

Specific to empowerment, it's simply not enough to obtain input and ideas from your employees. Good ideas are nothing more than that; they are ideas that offer no value if they are never capitalized upon. In this final chapter, I want to provide you with the specific impetus that will allow you to build and support a more empowered operation. It's not as much the ideas and approaches that are important as it is the process and persistence in attaining your desired outcomes that will yield the results you desire.

In this chapter I want to help you form a plan that will allow you to put together the pieces of the puzzle for your organization, business unit, or association in order to build an effective and sustainable operation. Think of this as the assembly of a fine watch. You can throw together a plastic Timex watch hoping the sale of which will yield enough revenue to justify its existence, or you can carefully craft a timeless brand such as Rolex that will not only stand out in the market as distinct, but contains enduring quality and a competitive advantage like no other.

There's an old saying, "Tell me and I forget. Show me and I may remember. Involve me and I learn."

If you've been paying attention throughout this book, you will have noticed an underlying theme. If you focus on capturing the minds of your employees, (that is, tapping into and using their collective knowledge and expertise), you inadvertently capture their hearts and in turn their commitment to the company, its customers, and its mission. The more you can involve employees in the business, the more committed they will be to the business.

What's Next: Using Empowerment to Improve Your Business, Your Team, and You

Many of the CEOs and business owners that I interact with face momentous challenges on a weekly, daily, and even hourly basis, all of which can be categorized into four buckets:

1. Business growth:
   - Improve brand awareness and reputation
   - Market more effectively
   - Sell more at higher margins
   - Satisfy and retain existing customers
   - Invest in mergers and acquisitions that enhance profitability
2. Business performance:
   - Formulating and achieving the business vision
   - Improving operational performance to create a competitive advantage
   - Reducing overhead to improve profitability
   - Investing in new technology and equipment for greater productivity
3. Stakeholder management:
   - Satisfying needs and demands of board members

- Satisfying and sourcing investors
- Satisfying needs of commercial investors
- Seeking and working with strategic partners

4. Employee performance:
   - Motivating and aligning leadership in support of strategy, performance, and stakeholder needs
   - Motivating employees to higher levels of performance to support these objectives
   - Engaging employees to obtain their commitment to the business and its mission
   - Nurturing increasing levels of employee performance

What you will have noticed throughout this book is that we have touched on virtually every point under "employee performance" above, with the exception of "nurturing increasing levels of employee performance." This was not an accident.

The logical question then becomes where to begin this journey to build recognizable and sustainable progress that can be measured against results. Here are the predominant considerations in priority sequence as they pertain to your business.

Beginning Your Empowerment Journey

As a car fanatic, I was recently watching the show *Street Outlaws*. Despite the danger that street racing presents (they are actually not on public streets, by the way), I found it interesting when one of the drivers explained that despite the excitement that a car wheelstanding off the starting line can present, it's actually one of the worst things a driver could ask for, not only because of the danger it presents (it's pretty difficult to drive while the front end is in midair), but because a car that wheelstands actually travels a farther distance than a car that does not. In essence, the car that makes it to the finish line first is the car that finds the shortest route there (where all other things remain equal).

I thought this explanation was quite profound because it also underlies the key to any successful organizational change initiative. Finding the shortest route with the least resistance is the key to ensuring rapid results. When this theory is applied to building a more empowered operation, there are some key considerations to reflect upon if you are to ensure quick and sustained success.

An Inclusive Direction

Are your employees at all levels of the business clear on the vision for the future of the company? More important, are they aware of why this vision is so crucial? If you haven't spent time educating employees on the environment, vision, and strategic objectives that the company is currently pursuing, then you have missed the most crucial step to forming an empowered operation—the "why":

- Why are we pursuing a future vision that is different from where the company is today?
- Why do we do the things we do when we do them?
- Why are we introducing so many changes to how we do things?
- Why don't we leave well enough alone?
- Why are our competitors nipping at our heels?

Your vision and strategy underlie (or at least should underlie—refer to Chapter 4) everything that you do, and if your employees don't know or can't connect with your strategy, then you are facing an uphill battle. Begin with the "why" so that you can quickly transition to the "what."

Let Employees Be Productive

Nearly a decade ago, in my corporate life, my employee Todd was disappointed to hear that I was transferring to another department after I had received a promotion. When I told him of the transition, he said, "That's too bad, Shawn, because I have enjoyed working with you—you deal with all of the (insert profanity here) and let me do what I am supposed to do—my job." This message has stuck with me ever since that day, and it is something that I have validated with dozens if not hundreds of other employees and leaders since. Employees want to be productive; they want to get their job done as efficiently and effectively as possible. What stands in their way? In most cases its pain.

I'm not referring to the pain of rejecting change, but the pain of continuously adapting to changes that haven't been completely thought out, or that haven't been aligned with the optimum way of doing things:

- ERP solutions that create extra keystrokes without demonstrating additional value for the effort
- Equipment that doesn't function as it was intended, forcing employees to take shortcuts
- Processes that improve functionality in one area but create obstacles and hindrances in another
- Lack of sufficient resources such as tools or technology
- Ineffective workspaces that add unnecessary movement or transport

The list is endless, and it only takes a few conversations with employees to understand where these pain points exist, and more important to gain ideas and solutions to alleviate the pain.

Take Action on Employee Ideas

I'm going to bet that if you spend any amount of time interacting with your employees, regardless of their level, position, or tenure in the company, your employees will present new ideas every day. These might include how to introduce a new product, how to improve an existing process, what new technology it makes sense to invest in, or even how to adjust existing reporting structures for greater levels of autonomy and effectiveness. The ideas themselves are plentiful, or at least they should be. What are leaders across your company doing with the gems that your employees provide?

Consider for a moment that the laws of atrophy suggest that if something isn't growing, it's decaying. How long can ideas from an employee fall on deaf ears before the motivation to continue to introduce new ideas wanes? Would you, faced with the prospect of your ideas being dismissed, ignored, or not acted upon, continue to offer new and innovative ideas to improve the performance of the business? Do you? The answer I would surmise is a resounding no.

Fortunately, if this is the environment you're in, there is hope. As human beings we are both forgiving and forgetful. (After all, why do you think politicians are voted in after making highly unpopular decisions?) Ignore my ideas for long, and I may stop offering them. Begin to take actions toward pursuing and introducing my new ideas, and I will quickly come around. I've experienced this time and again through various forums such as facilitated innovation sessions and during the formulation of strategy. Even the most deterred or disgruntled employees will come around if and when they begin to see ideas acted upon.

Find a way to begin to solicit ideas from your employees, and then place them into processes that facilitate their review, prioritization, and, most important, implementation. You need not act on every idea to instill a desire for employees to contribute, but there must be a continued demonstration of ideas being introduced, or action that results from ideas that employees have suggested, if you are going to win over their minds and hearts.

Build Strength in Your Community

As you begin to build confidence, commitment, and momentum in empowering your organization, there will invariably be employees that do not fit your mold as your community grows. What should you do with these employees? The first consideration is that employees themselves do not evolve on a continuum; that is, not all employees will buy into or support your approach to empowerment at the same time. As I suggested at the beginning of this book, building an empowered community is not a quick fix or a light switch. It takes time and sustained effort to begin to experience the quantifiable results I've referred to throughout this book. More on this in a moment.

Eliminate Your DUDs

At this point I will acknowledge that within your organization (and virtually every other organization that exists today), there are going to be employees or even business leaders who are not progressing at all; they don't buy into your vision, they don't support the evolution of the business, and they avoid participating in the steadily forming community and subcommunities. In fact, they often refuse to contribute or participate at all. I call these employees DUDs—which stands for: Don't Understand, Don't care. (Notice how communication once again is a component of the poorest-performing employees. Even the most disengaged employees are forced to care to an extent when they truly understand the organization's vision, direction, challenges, and opportunities, and their role in support of such.)

Every company has some DUDs, and I would be remiss if I didn't speak to them at some point. What truly sets apart an empowered operation (and a high-performing business) is the willingness to stay the journey and slowly eliminate the DUDs from the organization. If you choose instead to toe the line and continue to try (and try, and try) to bring them along, you're simply wasting your time, their time, and the time of other employees who are committed and engaged. Take rapid action to assist DUDs in finding connection with the company and its community, or send them packing. Otherwise they will distract you and derail you from evolving into an empowered operation. Harsh? Maybe. Necessary? Absolutely.

Strengthen Recruitment

In addition to eliminating DUDs, you will lose some employees through natural attrition (although you will lose fewer employees if you truly build an empowered community); therefore, to build strength it's important to consider your recruitment practices. It's natural to look for "the right candidate" for a role within a company by considering prospective employees' experience, qualifications, and expertise, but what about their fit within the existing community? In a recent conversation with Kate Ahrens, vice president of Flying Colors, I learned that the motto for hiring within her company is simple: "Come with the right attitude and we will help you attain the skills you need." Skills can be taught; attitude cannot. Incorporating aspects of assessing "fit" against your empowered community in recruitment practices will assist you in continuing to build strength as attrition occurs.

Capitalize on Your Community

As subcommunities—smaller communities within the broader community that contain like-minded individuals with common objectives in support of the broader company vision—begin to form within your organization, it's essential that you capitalize on the positive momentum to support further strengthening of empowerment. These subcommunities can take the form of groups dedicating their personal time in support of a charity such as Walk for Cancer,[1] groups that meet during off-hours for fitness classes and events, or even groups that connect outside of work hours in order to pursue a hobby of mutual interest. A close friend of mine, Jeremy, is an avid kayaker, having connected with a small group with similar interests during his time working at his previous employer. Despite moving on to work in another organization, he still meets with the other kayak enthusiasts on a monthly basis, a group that has been meeting now for over five years.

The power in subcommunities is that they are like-minded individuals who have two things in common. First they all share a common interest in the same hobby, charity, or other group. Second, they all initially connected or met as a result of working within the same organization. As the "career connection" exists, it provides an opportunity for a company to further strengthen its support of employees by nurturing these subcommunities, thereby increasing the appreciation and recognition of the company itself. For example, a friend organized a walk for a charity at her company. Once the group had critical mass of people to participate, she approached senior management to ask for a donation toward their charity. Senior management, recognizing the power of supporting subcommunities within the company, in turn escalated the request to the CEO, who not only offered a financial contribution that far outweighed that of any other charity the business supported, but promoted the event and charity to all employees in the company's employee newsletter, further increasing exposure of the charity (which increased donations) and the company's support of its employees. The effect snowballed from there as spouses who received the newsletter told others, who in turn contributed even though they didn't work at the company. Media exposure followed, which once again increased donations outside the company.

The benefit to those who organized support for the charity was having a higher donation than any other team that participated. The benefit to the company was the display of its support of employees, which appealed to other employees outside the company, who in turn began to watch for openings to work with the business. This is employee attraction at work, all as a result of supporting and capitalizing on subcommunities that exist within the organization.

Tools for Empowered Operational Success

With these considerations in mind, there are also some important tools to assist in your empowered operations journey. Having a plan to build a new home may be all that is needed to break ground, but without the right tools and continuous measurement against the plan, it's impossible to ensure that the home that is built is the one you intended.

Formulate a Plan

Success in forming an empowered operation results from formulating a plan with a clear beginning and a vision of success. Formulating a plan requires asking the following questions:

1. Where should we begin: what are the greatest gaps in the company today?
2. How should we begin: what approach will yield the greatest chance for success?
3. When should we begin: what is the right time to begin considering other existing initiatives?

A plan is not something that is conceived in isolation. (If that's what you're thinking, I suggest you review Chapter 3.) By collaborating with senior leaders and employees on formulation of the plan, you will build a robust yet pragmatic approach to beginning the journey of empowerment.

Determine Pit Stops

With a plan in place, the logical next step is to ascertain what success will look like at critical points in the journey. For example, if you determine that incorporating employee feedback into the formulation of your business strategy is a critical first step, then consider what success will look like for you and for the business in doing so. What are the different outcomes you expect to achieve as a result of including their feedback? Will it be easier to introduce the strategy to the broader organization? If so, how? Setting pit stops, as I like to call them, is critical to ensuring you achieve your desired outcomes. You must also allow for adjustments in the event your plan is not heading in the direction you had expected.

Adopt Measures of Success

With pit stops identified, how will you measure success to ensure that judgment, although relevant, is not the only factor by which you measure success? At every pit stop and critical juncture in your journey, it's important to stop and consider whether you are where you intended to be. This is not to say that a different outcome is a bad outcome. Most executives and business owners that I know consider key performance indicators (KPIs) as set in stone, which is wrong. The reality is it can be very difficult to identify what success (in the form of a KPI) will look like until you reach the destination. For this reason I prefer to set measures of success, which include a combination of both quantitative and qualitative outcomes, and offer less stringency in identifying what success will look like.

The most common measures result from considering the following questions:

1. What is the desired specific outcome?
2. What would a successful outcome look like and feel like to achieve?
3. How would you know you've achieved success at this juncture?

For every pit stop set at least one measure of success to assist you in ascertaining whether you are on the right path to success.

Optimize Your Speed

As I alluded to at the beginning of this book, forming an empowered operation is not a quick fix or an overnight solution, although incorporating even small elements of the approaches and concepts I've discussed would go a long way to helping improve the performance of your organization and its operation. It's critical to consider the speed with which you approach forming a more empowered operation. As the saying goes, Rome wasn't built in a day; hence this is a journey that requires patience, persistence, and persuasiveness (the three keys to success). It's entirely possible that it won't be until your second strategy that you achieve the desired engagement and empowerment from your employees. After all, if you are to tap into your employees for input into the future of the business, something that you've never actually done before, it's entirely possible that employees won't provide you forthright and valuable information until they have seen their initial input incorporated and acted upon. Empowerment in any form requires trust, and trust takes time.

What I suggest to my clients is that you have to moderate your speed. Push hard for results and you in turn will diminish trust. Drag your heels at taking action toward employee ideas and input, and you will erode existing trust. There is an optimum speed to pursue your plan, and that speed will become increasingly relevant once you tune in and listen to employees. Are they buying into and taking action on your desire to engage and empower them, or are many of them sitting back and waiting to see what happens?

The key point here? Too fast is just as bad as too slow. Stay attuned to employee feedback, actions, and reactions, and you will find the optimum velocity for your journey.

Reward Failure

To fail means to try. As you begin to empower employees in various aspects of your plan, the question is not *if* there will be failure, but when. The answer is in how you and other business leaders respond to the failure. I mentioned the empowered operational journey of Mike Vokes of Vokes Furniture earlier in the book. Early in his journey, Mike empowered one of his team leaders to make decisions on which customer orders were shipped each day. After several months it became apparent that outbound shipments were not being coordinated as effectively as they could, resulting in congestion in the shipping and staging areas of the plant, despite several discussions with the employee empowered to complete the task. What did Mike do? He held a meeting between the team leaders to ensure they met daily to review customer orders to be shipped to ensure outbound freight would be better organized in order to meet customer demands and satisfy floor space requirements. Mike didn't overreact and delegate the task to someone else. He took the proactive steps to ensure that his company's journey to operational empowerment continued.

Failures and mistakes are bound to happen as you hand over greater control and decision-making power to employees. What's critical is not the failure itself, but how you respond or react to the failure. One false move, reaction, or statement in what you are trying to achieve can quickly extinguish all of your work to date. Thomas Edison failed 700 times to create the lightbulb before finding the best solution. The key is to reward and celebrate failures, as they confirm that everyone is trying something different and something new; it's through trying that we find new and better ways of achieving our desired outcomes. A mistake is only a mistake if it happens more than once.

Common Mistakes, Pitfalls, and Missteps in an Empowered Operational Journey

With our discussions turning to failures and mistakes, I want to spend a few minutes discussing some of the pitfalls and challenges that I've encountered in supporting executives and business owners in further empowering their operation. Before doing so, it's important to ensure that you are clear on the last point above; that failure in some way, shape, or form is to be expected, but it's how you respond to the failure that sets apart an empowered operation versus any other business.

If you've read this book in its entirety, then you know that I've mentioned some of these points before. This said, it's crucial that I reaffirm their possible existence, as I want to highlight the fact that this journey, if you choose to take it, will not necessarily be the path that other organizations have taken. The main reason for this is that it is a journey; it takes time and hard work, as does anything in business that is worth its outcome.

Here are some of the most common missteps and mistakes I've encountered:

> **Too much too fast.** I've mentioned this point several times during this last chapter, but I simply can't reinforce it enough. Speed kills. If you try to approach this journey without a plan and a realistic timeline to success, you are more likely to harm your organization than help it. Your speed must be governed to ensure that this is not seen as "just another initiative" by employees, and that you are prepared to make the changes necessary to capitalize on your efforts. Pushing too hard for results and outcomes turns employees off no differently than taking too much time to think about or consider the risks of taking any action at all.
>
> **Diminishing revenue and market share.** If your business is quickly losing ground, (that is, you are losing market share and/or revenue), then focus your efforts in the short-term on boosting sales. Building an empowered operation requires time and in some instances money. If you lack either or both, there will be more pressure to increase the speed by which you achieve results, and

you are likely to fall into the trap I identified above. There is no doubt that an empowered operation is one that will ensure continued business growth, new opportunities, and new markets. If you are already facing cash-flow problems, however, focus your energy on fixing them before you worry about shifting how your business operates.

Isolated incidents. Forming an empowered operation requires a plan with the intention of building a better business and a stronger community. Deciding that you are going to incorporate the views and ideas of employees in a single area while ignoring them in another sends mixed messages, and once again diminishes trust in the eyes of employees. Create a plan that encompasses all of the elements I have discussed in this book to ensure that you are taking a robust and sustained approach.

Lack of executive support. I spent an entire chapter (Chapter 3) discussing this point, but it's so crucial I have to mention it again. This is not something that one person or a couple people can accomplish. If members of your board or executive team are against forming a more empowered operation, then it is likely you will fail. Delays in making decisions and taking actions will slow your progress, which in turn will impact employee trust and your efforts. This is an all-in approach to forming a stronger business, and it requires support at the highest levels of the business.

Heavy-handed labor practices. I would be remiss if I didn't mention organized labor at some point in this book. I've had my share of experiences working with organized labor unions both as an executive and as a consultant. The reality that I've found time and again is that the single greatest barrier to reaching common ground between management and a union is the actual or perceived lack of trust that exists between the parties. This takes time to overcome, hence it takes more time in your empowered operational journey. This isn't to say that labor practices should deter you from shifting how you operate your business. They should, however, reinforce the idea that velocity is critical to success. It is likely to take longer to agree on directions and reach intended outcomes when unions are involved, until trust has been established or strengthened.

"Try and see" approach. The concepts we have discussed in this book are quite straightforward, but also quite complex. It takes time and tenacity to change the direction of an organization; hence building a more empowered operation requires an "all-in" approach. As I outlined above, it's simply illogical to think that you can change one thing and then see what happens before you move ahead. This said, the very reason pit stops are necessary is to ensure you are on the right track before proceeding. A poor pit stop doesn't mean you throw in the towel and resign from the race, though. Create a robust plan and set milestones and pit stops with the intent of ensuring continued progress. If your intent is anything otherwise, I would suggest that you aren't truly ready to build an empowered operation.

The Evolution of Operational Empowerment: The Next Generation

As we wrap up, I want to take a moment to discuss the evolution of operational empowerment. Clearly, the pace of change continues to increase, and from an organizational standpoint we are making decisions and incorporating changes on a daily basis faster than any time in history. There are a couple of key points to consider moving forward, as they possess significant influence in how businesses will operate in the future, and the future isn't as far away as you might think.

If you've spent time researching the future generations of leaders and owners of businesses, it's clear that generation Y and generation Z (as they are commonly referred to at the writing of this book) have a very different way of looking at the world and a different way in which they choose to work. Despite the complexities of this topic, I want to focus on a couple of key points relative to our discussion.

1. **Social revolution.** The advent of social media and other technologies has clearly influenced how we—and in particular the younger

generations who have grown up with these technologies—think, respond, and behave. It's not uncommon for younger generations of employees today to have intimate friendships with individuals from around the world whom they've never met face to face. And what do they talk about? They discuss what their jobs are like, what their companies are like, and what their bosses are like. When you consider that gen Y is the most highly educated generation ever to enter the workforce, the question that you have to consider is whether members of this generation are smarter than you. They lack experience, yes, but they also lack an understanding or buy-in to bureaucracy, and returning to the very first chapter in this book, the current organizational and management structure that many businesses operate under is highly bureaucratic.

If Gen Y employees don't feel included in decisions relative to the future of the business, its direction, or customers, chances are they will find another company that does, or simply start their own. More important, they will be sure to share their thoughts about your company and its lack of empowerment practices with anyone and everyone who connects with them socially and online.

Therefore, if you're unsure that this is the right approach for your business, I am going to boldly suggest to you that empowerment is the only way in which you will attract and retain gen Y and gen Z employees. This said, your business is about to transition whether you like it or not, so by following the premise and ideas contained within this book you will be taking a proactive approach to capturing the best talent and building an operation that has a significant competitive advantage over your competition—that is, if your competition is still around.

2. **Social influence**. Building on my points above, all generations today are becoming more socially aware and adept. We have grown accustomed to sharing our ideas, thoughts, and opinions publically, which means that we expect to be able to do the same within our companies, and—as a result of tools such as "likes" and

"shares"—we expect to be heard. If you fail to listen to, respond to, and act on the ideas and suggestions of your employees, which is at the heart of empowerment, then you are unlikely in future years to have any employees—or at least the type of employees you prefer to have—remaining.

Notes

Introduction

1. Harvard Business Review. 2011. *Harvard Business Review Aligning Technology with Strategy*. Harvard Business Review Press.

Chapter 1

1. Accountemps. 2013. *Survey: Human resources managers cite lack of communication as main source of low employee morale.*
2. Gallup. 2013. *State of the global workplace.*
3. Langfield, Amy. 2013. *McDonalds finance guide insulting to low wage workers.* CNBC.
4. Connect + Develop is a registered service mark of Procter & Gamble.

Chapter 2

1. Hofstede, G. 1991. *Cultures and organizations: Software of the mind.*
2. The Conference Board, Inc. 2013. *The conference board, CEO challenge® 2013.*
3. Gallup. 2013. *State of the American workplace.*
4. Stelter, B. 2011. *Netflix, in reversal, will keep its services together.* The New York Times.

Chapter 3

1. Peter Drucker was an Austrian-born American management consultant, educator, and author.
2. Moxie Software is a provider of chat, email, and knowledge transfer software.
3. Hill, C., G. Jones, and M. Schilling. 2014. *Strategic management theory: An integrated approach.*
4. Albert-László Barabási, Romanian-born Hungarian-American physicist; best known for his work in the research of network theory.
5. Catmull, Dr. E. 2014. *Creativity, Inc.: Overcoming the unseen forces that stand in the way of true inspiration.* Bantam Press.
6. Maslow, A. 1943. *A Theory of Human Motivation.* Psychological Review 50(4):370–96.
7. U.S. Department of Labor. 2012. *Statistical abstract of the United States.*
8. Gallup. 2013. *State of the American workplace.*
9. Toro Company. http://www.toro.com/en-ca/about-us/Pages/employees-and-culture.aspx.

Chapter 4

1. Albert S. Humphrey was an American business and management consultant who specialized in organizational management and cultural change.

2. *12 Angry Men* (1957), a movie drama by Sidney Lumet.
3. The Economist. 2013. *Why good strategies fail: Lessons for the C-Suite.*
4. Dr. John Kotter, a well-known thought leader in the fields of business, leadership, and change.
5. Ottinger, R. 2012. *Failed strategy execution due to oversight by corporate boards?*
6. Thompson, D. 2012. *War and peace in 30 seconds: How much does the military spend on ads?* The Atlantic.

Chapter 5

1. Kotter, J. 1996. *Leading change.* Harvard Business Review Press.
2. Hamel, G., and M. Zanini. 2014. *Build a change platform, not a change program.* McKinsey & Company.
3. Dew, J. R., and M. M. Nearing. 2004. *Continuous quality improvement in higher education.* Praeger Publishers Inc.
4. http://www.britannica.com/topic/Encarta.
5. Batten, M. C. *A History of Associations.* CSAE.
6. Tuttle, B. 2013. *The 5 big mistakes that led to Ron Johnson's ouster at JC Penney.* Time.

Chapter 6

1. Robert Browning was an English poet and playwright.
2. The Conference Board, Inc. 2013. *The conference board, CEO challenge® 2013.*

Chapter 7

1. https://en.wikipedia.org/wiki/United_Breaks_Guitars.
2. https://en.wikipedia.org/wiki/Zappos.
3. https://en.wikipedia.org/wiki/Where%27s_the_beef%3F.
4. Hsieh, T. 2013. *Delivering happiness: A path to profits, passion, and purpose.* Grand Central Publishing.
5. Hsieh, T. 2013. *Delivering happiness: A path to profits, passion, and purpose.* Grand Central Publishing.

Chapter 8

1. http://www.scdigest.com/ASSETS/ON_TARGET/12-07-27-1.php.
2. https://www.atkearney.com/news-media/news-releases/news-release/-/asset_publisher/00OIL7Jc67KL/content/more-than-half-of-the-automotive-supply-base-could-go-bankrupt-in-2009-at-least-1-million-job-losses-expected/10192.
3. http://www.emd-performance-materials.com/en/coatings/coatings_xirallic/coatings_xirallic.html.

Chapter 10

1. https://en.wikipedia.org/wiki/Innovation.
2. http://www.fastcompany.com/most-innovative-companies/2014/dropbox.
3. https://en.wikipedia.org/wiki/Uber_%28company%29.

Chapter 11

1. https://en.wikipedia.org/wiki/Post-it_note.
2. https://en.wikipedia.org/wiki/Procter_%26_Gamble.

Chapter 12

1. http://www.cancer.org/involved/participate/relayforlife/.

Index